Human Security and Sierra Leone's Post-Conflict Development

Human Security and Sierra Leone's Post-Conflict Development

Francis Wiafe-Amoako
Foreword by Ali A. Mazrui

LEXINGTON BOOKS
Lanham • Boulder • New York • London

Published by Lexington Books
An imprint of The Rowman & Littlefield Publishing Group, Inc.
4501 Forbes Boulevard, Suite 200, Lanham, Maryland 20706
www.rowman.com

16 Carlisle Street, London W1D 3BT, United Kingdom

British Library Cataloguing in Publication Information Available

Library of Congress Cataloging-in-Publication Data

Wiafe-Amoako, Francis, author.
Human security and Sierra Leone's post-conflict development / Francis Wiafe-Amoako.
pages cm.
Includes bibliographical references and index.
ISBN 978-0-7391-9133-0 (cloth : alk. paper) — ISBN 978-0-7391-9134-7 (electronic)
1. Human security—Sierra Leone. 2. Sierra Leone—Social conditions—1961– 3. Sierra Leone—History—Civil War, 1991–2002—Peace. 4. Postwar reconstruction—Sierra Leone. 5. Sierra Leone—History—21st century. I. Title.
JC599.S425W53 2014
966.405—dc23
2014020217

™ The paper used in this publication meets the minimum requirements of American National Standard for Information Sciences Permanence of Paper for Printed Library Materials, ANSI/NISO Z39.48-1992.

Printed in the United States of America

Mom
Comfort Amoako (aka Auntie Esi Kraba)

Dad
Yaw Lawrence Amoako

Contents

Foreword

Ali A. Mazrui

This volume by Francis Wiafe-Amoako signifies the fourth wave of post-colonial political literature. The first wave was very optimistic about the unfolding post-colonial narrative. Africa's founding fathers believed paradoxically both in resurrecting older values and in innovation and experimentation. Let us examine the different phases of political change.

I. THE PHASE OF INNOVATION

The first years of Africa's independence were accompanied by relative self-confidence. The first generation of African decision-makers were opening new doors and seeking new horizons. A particularly ambitious experiment was that of Julius K. Nyerere's African route to Socialism. Nyerere called this Ujamaa: The Basis of African Socialism. Nyerere's approach included collective responsibility for such vulnerable groups as the elderly, the poor, the sick, the disabled, and the very young. Nyerere implemented a form of Socialism in the villages—what was called "ujamaa vijijini."

Other regimes or political movements in post-colonial Africa were less convincing than Nyerere when they claimed to be "socialist." Rhetorical "socialists" included Léopold Sédar Senghor of Senegal and Sékou Touré of Guinea. Another area of experimentation in those early years of post-independence was the one-party state. Kwame Nkrumah of Ghana was among the first to experiment with the single party. The Ivory Coast under Félix Houphouët-Boigny also experimented. Julius Nyerere set up a committee to evaluate the case for a constitutional one-party state.

Nkrumah's rationale for a single-party democracy was almost the opposite of the situation in Nyerere's Tanzania. Nkrumah argued that post-colonial Ghana was too divided to be able to risk a multi-party system. On the other hand, post-colonial Tanzania illustrated that the country was too united to produce a viable opposition party. The country's last post-colonial election produced such an overwhelming majority support for the ruling party (TANU) that the Opposition consisted of only a single Member of Parliament.

II. THE PHASE OF DESTABILIZATION

This second stage of post-colonial history witnessed the early phases of destabilization. Ethnic rivalry became a major challenge to political stability. Another area of instability consists of civil-military relations. There have been multiple studies of why military coups occur in some African countries and not in others. Coup-prone countries in the first fifty years of Africa's independence included Nigeria, Ghana, Burkina Faso, the two Congoes (Kinshasa and Brazzaville) and the three Guineas (French, Portuguese, and Spanish). African states which have been coup-proof have included Zambia, Malawi, Tanzania, Senegal, South Africa, and, most surprising of all, Zimbabwe, in spite of economic and political collapse. Had Zimbabwe been in West Africa it might have had a military coup before the thirtieth year of independence (the year 2010).

III. THE PHASE OF POLITICAL COLLAPSE

This post-colonial stage can mean a civil war in an African country. Tyranny means too much government—whereas anarchy means too little government. In Idi Amin's Uganda there was both tyranny and anarchy. When either tyranny or anarchy goes too far we have a failed state. A civil war may be a quarrel over resources or a clash of racial or ethnic identities. Somalia became a failed state after experiencing first tyranny, and then anarchy. The Somali anarchy even included piracy on the high seas. The failed state of Sierra Leone and of Congo (Kinshasa) has been neither a rational scramble for resources nor a clash of emotional identities. Both Sierra Leone and the larger Congo have deteriorated into anarchy, rape, and conflict. These were ruthless abuses of power in both countries. Sierra Leone especially has tried to find long-term solutions.

IV. THE POST-CONFLICT PHASE

This book by Francis Wiafe-Amoako opens up the fourth phase of post-conflict African situations. The search continues for directions and for sharing power. Wiafe-Amoako distrusts the idea of power-sharing. He is right that power-sharing without trust is a prescription for failure. As Africa continues this search for building stronger and trustworthy societies and states, developing institutions that support human security are in the right direction.

Ali A. Mazrui, D.Phil., (Oxon), C.B.S.
Albert Schweitzer Professor in the Humanities
Director, Institute for Global Cultural Studies
Binghamton University (SUNY)

Preface

At the background of this book is the development of appropriate institutions to ensure stable after-conflict environments for states coming out of violent conflicts. States that have undergone violent conflicts continue to be fragile, and they threaten the security of their own people and the geographical region to which they belong. It is not uncommon to observe that the prescription for stabilizing these after-conflict states has been to put in place electoral democracy. Elections have the effect of stabilizing the existing tense political environment. When elections fail to achieve the needed stability, power-sharing agreement has been applied.

This book re-emphasizes the need to understand the context within which conflict occurs, which is critical to finding a sustainable peace. Understanding conflicts make each conflict unique and challenges the prescription of common solutions for all conflicts. In addition, conflicts become violent and protracted when parties are unable to find common ground. This common ground reflects the perceived outcome of the negotiated settlement. Conflicts arise out of the sense that needs are not met; there are feelings of exclusion and marginalization. Crafting a post-conflict peace strategy should not just focus on developmental strategy but also institutions that ensure human dignity. This makes human security key to conflict management in general and the post-conflict in particular. An all-encompassing approach to conflict management needs to be the strategy in addressing contemporary conflicts. In addition to helping to achieve sustainable after-conflict environment, human security could assist in reducing humanitarian crisis, alleviate pressure on global finance, and ensure peace and development. This book proposes a human-centered approach at resolving conflict. Merely organizing elections under the pretense of resolving conflict needs to be re-examined. It is well established that dictators have used and continue to use elections to justify their perpetual stay in power. The elections process has, thus, not reduced the insecurities within states.

A human security approach to conflict management has lasting consequences. Not only does it ensure security and human dignity to the people, it also ensures political consolidation, peace, and survival for political leaders. Political elites in the developing world are greatly concerned about life after political office and, therefore, want to hold on to power as long as they can. Human security ensures a secured environment that elites can also enjoy when they are out of public office. This is a good reason to incentivize political elites to seek to establish institutions that promote human security whiles they are in office.

Sierra Leone's post-conflict environment is faced with tremendous challenges. Several of the policy reforms are in the right direction. However, its leaders should not lose focus in making sure that the dignity of the Sierra Leonean people is assured at the end of the day.

Acknowledgments

In writing this maiden book, I have treaded the journey with caution, sometimes not sure of how treacherous the critiques out there will be. Coming this far would not have been possible without certain accomplished individuals whose encouragements have been invaluable.

My appreciation goes to Professor Ali A. Mazrui for writing the foreword to this book. Regardless of his international commitments, he made time to read the manuscript and offered suggestions.

I recognize the contribution of Professor Luis Benjamim Serapiao, professor of conflict resolution and African studies at Howard University, for reading the manuscript and making critical comments regarding the conflict management process. I also want to recognize Professor Sulaymann Nyang for his moral support and encouragement throughout my student life and beyond. His review of this manuscript and suggestions are invaluable and very much appreciated.

I want to commend Dr. Cynthia Adom-Portuphy and Dr. Edwin Oyoo for taking the time off their busy schedules to proofread and edit this work.

I am also indebted to my wife, Agnes, for her support along this journey. Besides her encouragement and moral support, she has been around to take care of our three lovely children (Francisca, Stephen, and Aneesah) while I traveled around in search of data to complete this work.

Chapter One

Introduction

Post-conflict reconstruction[1] and development has become a household phenomenon within the cycles of international development. In Africa,[2] the term cannot be relevant and real enough as a spate of conflict and other forms of instability engulf the continent. Post-conflict reconstruction is associated with multiple and complex policies and strategies to stabilize and secure states that have recently undergone violent conflicts. Policymakers and other stakeholders interested in these post-conflict states however face challenges as to where to begin in trying to stabilize these states. One of the reasons why policymakers struggle is how to draw the line between post-conflict reconstruction and strategies needed for normal development. Are these two the same and could they be achieved at the same time? After violent conflict, the last thing people in those states need is to be told to wait a little longer for the benefit of development strategies that have been or are being put in place to kick in so their well-being could be improved. People in post-conflict states need jobs and opportunities; but, most importantly, they need a secured environment that ensures an adequate amount of trust[3] at both the state and community levels. This book identifies human security as a fundamental piece of the post-conflict era. It notes that any strategy to achieve stability and development in the post-conflict must consciously incorporate elements of human security.

A secured environment has generally been conducive to development and stable societies. Many developed states are comparatively stable to developing states. Societies have pursued secured environments to ensure continuity of life, self-fulfillment, and development. Thomas Hobbes,[4] and later John Locke[5] in his social contract theory, set out the terms with which people within societies could forge compromises that could enhance their own personal securities and enable development. In his hypothetical state of nature,

Hobbes noted that life in a state of nature is poor, brutish, and short, and that this all-out war between people could be averted if everyone submitted their freedom to the state or a central government in the form of a social contract. The state, which is assumed to be powerful, or an absolute sovereign, would then use its power to create an enabling environment for all to be secure in their personal lives and to pursue their individual potential abilities. However, several states in post-independent Africa, and especially in the period after the Cold War, have failed to create a safe and enabling environment for their people. Some states have become predatory states or "Frankenstein" as scholars like Ali A. Mazrui[6] will note regarding the nature of the state reflected by the actions and policies pursued by the ruling elites. The ruling elites have succeeded in using the state's resources to intimidate and scare its own people. Sierra Leone, for example, has been plagued with political instability since 1967. In the process, a full-blown civil conflict ensued in 1991 until it was officially declared ended in 2002. The conflict resulted in loss of many lives and properties, displacement of over two million Sierra Leoneans, and continued retrogression in economic development.

UNDERSTANDING INTERNAL CONFLICTS

The proliferation of internal conflict in countries such as Sierra Leone has become an uncontrollable endemic reality. It is as if, by default, the very nature of the society warrants such conflicts. This phenomenon has reached a level where it does not even surprise the outside world, and even Africans themselves, when a new internal conflict arises in any of these African states. The recruitment and mobilization of rebel forces and the intensity of combat in such domestic conflicts need further analysis in the field of peace and conflict studies. It reflects a much deeper institutional weakness and the inability of the state to secure domestic peace. These sudden and intense conflict situations are in sharp contrast to the euphoria that engulfed the African people and the entire continent in the days prior, and immediately following the struggles for independence. Like in many other African states, the initial disagreements between the Krios and the Protectorate[7] were resolved with the absorption of moderate Krios into the Sierra Leone Peoples Party (SLPP).[8] With the adoption of the Constitution in 1951, the way was cleared for the final push for general elections in November of 1951 and subsequent independence in April of 1961. The spirit of nationalism has dissipated in the post-colonial era. Africa has not been spared conflicts in the latter parts of the twentieth, and well into the twenty-first centuries. Aside from Sierra Leone, violent conflicts in countries such as the Democratic Republic of Congo (DRC), Angola, Liberia, Rwanda, Burundi, Central

African Republic, Mali, and Cote D'Ivoire still bring nightmarish memories to people both closer to, and far from these conflict areas.

Internal conflicts in Africa sometimes overwhelm African leaders who may, in some cases, not know how these conflicts started[9] or how to resolve or manage the conflict situation. In Sierra Leone for instance, political leaders from Siaka Stevens to Ahmed Tejan Kabbah often relied on one ethnic group to oppress or marginalize other groups as a means to hold on to power and ensure some form of "political stability."[10] These strategies to conflict resolution have failed to produce stable and secured environments. Sierra Leonean leaders, like many African leaders, realize the importance of secured environment in the development process; but non-existent, and sometimes ineffective institutions make it difficult, if not impossible, to achieve the needed security.

POST-CONFLICT RECONSTRUCTION AND THE LITERATURE ON CONFLICT ONSET IN AFRICA

Developing appropriate strategies and attitudes in the post-conflict era need an understanding of the origin of the cause of conflict. This is to prevent a one-size-fits-all approach at stabilizing these states to allow for sustainable peace and development to take place.

The literature on internal conflict in post-colonial Africa has focused on explaining the cause(s) of the proliferation of such conflicts.[11] The most dominant of these has attributed the causes of internal conflict to primordial sentiments. Primordialists argue that diverse ethnic identities (language, religion, or some form of cultural combinations) has been the most predominant cause of conflict in Africa; that ethnicity drives consciousness and creates an in-group/out-group cohesion necessary for the onset of conflict. Primordialists maintain that "clearly identifiable communities would prefer to be governed poorly or inefficiently by their own ethnic kind than they would otherwise be efficiently governed by people from other ethnicities."[12] Some ethnicities believe that it is degrading for them to be ruled by other ethnicities.[13] Explaining conflict from the Primordialist perspective literally rejects the concept of the state system. The assumption here is that people from different backgrounds cannot tolerate the notion that they have a common goal for self-determination and use their diverse skills and resources to work together for a common good. Dealing with the post-conflict from this perspective also suggests that the country should be split into different ethnicities or organized along ethnic lines—an approach which is hardly the case, and applied in very few countries in Africa such as Eritrea and South Sudan. Even in these states we still have problems of peace and securities. However, many policymakers and stakeholders appear to draft post-conflict reconstruction strategies with the Primordialist agenda in mind. In Ethiopia for instance, regional and ethnic parties have been formed as a means to ensure domestic political stability. In Sierra Leone, as in other African states, political parties have had strongholds in certain regions just because the leadership of those parties comes from those regions. Many have interpreted this to mean that because the leaders hail from that region that is why they have the support. However, underlying this idea is the issue of trust. Somalia's stability, from the Primordialist point of view, should not have posed any challenges at all due to the common cultures, language, and religion of the people. But post-conflict reconstruction and development in Somalia has been intractable and elusive.

Secondly, the level of economic development is also widely argued as a possible indicator for the onset of civil conflict, and that internal wars are motivated and sustained by the benefits that accrue from such conflicts.[14] Between 1992 and 1996, at the height of the civil war in Liberia, Charles Taylor made personal gains of US $400 million per year.[15] The "war economy" proposition also argues that the persistent war in the Democratic Republic of Congo (DRC) made neighboring states such as Rwanda and Uganda become major trade routes for informal trade networks and have become exporters of gold and cobalt even though such precious metals are not extracted from those two states.[16] This situation makes the interest of the neighboring states a critical issue in dealing with stability and development in the post-conflict states. In the Sierra Leonean case the rebels took over the southeastern region of the country, specifically the Kono region where the country's large diamond deposits are located. Not only did the RUF boost its funding and sustain the war, but the unemployed youth in the area got to have access to the nation's valuable resources they had been denied for a very long time. A reduction in economic development does not necessarily mean war is on the horizon since many African countries have been resilient and stayed secured in tough economic conditions. However, post-conflict strategies based on the economic explanations need to focus on the distribution and access to the nation's resources and other opportunities. In Nigeria's Delta region, the instability has been due to the lack of access and the equitable distribution of the oil resources, and environmental safety issues. Cabinda in Angola also faces the same problem. Thus, underlying these major arguments for conflict onset in Africa stems from the fact that some category of groups, either deliberately or unintentionally, have been marginalized or excluded from sharing in the political, social, and economic benefits of the state.[17] In addition to this, the lack of opportunities or outlets for marginalized groups to access and address their predicaments could breach weak domestic security systems and lead to instability. In the twentieth century, the Burundi and Rwandan cases are classic examples of the consequences of extreme marginalization and exclusions from participating in societal responsibilities. In the twenty-first century the Arab Spring is a classic example of what awaits leaders and states when an enabling space is not made available for people to realize their life goals.

The intensity of marginalization and exclusion creates a sense of threat to the livelihood of those that are discriminated against. Such threats that affect human lives and well-being are the basic cause for the proliferation of conflict in Africa.[18] When an identifiable group perceives a threat to its survival, there is the tendency for such marginalized groups to mobilize. Consequently, these groups fight back to regain their share of the national cake and to improve their chances for future survival. In the genocidal wars in Burundi and Rwanda, for instance, the majority Hutus believed that they were marginalized by the minority Tutsis during the colonial, and well into the post-independent era.

As the proliferation of internal conflicts threatens the internal security of the conflict state and its neighbors, efforts have been made to resolve or manage these conflicts and to prevent future occurrences. The default conflict management strategies in sub-Saharan Africa have mainly evolved around putting in place some sort of democratic process, culminating in the organization of elections and leaders selected by established electoral rules. In some limited cases, a power-sharing government has been put in place where cabinet positions are allocated among political factions based on some agreed-upon rules. In the Abidjan and Lome Peace Accords, the rebel group, Revolutionary United Front (RUF), was allocated some government positions and other privileges in some form of a power-sharing arrangement.[19] In Kenya, for instance, the disputed outcome of the December 2007 presidential and parliamentary elections between the incumbent president, Mwai Kibaki of the National Rainbow Coalition (NRC), and challenger, Raila Odinga of the Orange Democratic Movement (ODM), was resolved by the establishment of a coalition government (some form of a power-sharing deal). A new prime ministerial position was created to be occupied by Raila Odinga, and cabinet positions were accordingly allocated among the two parties. The Zimbabwean post-election conflict was also resolved using a power-sharing arrangement. Organizing elections, and sometimes supplementing the democratic process with power-sharing arrangements as strategies to achieve stable post-conflict environments, have had mixed results. Power sharing in Burundi has led to some relative stability in the country. However, power-sharing in Kenya and Zimbabwe led to protracted gridlock in government and created more insecurity in both states and a drag on development targets in the post-election conflict era.

Managing the post-conflict era in some sub-Saharan Africa countries has thus far proven elusive to stakeholders interested in conflict management in the region. Fragile state structures have mostly been the result. This is because post-conflict management strategies have failed to secure and promote human security.[20] The desired target of improving the lives of the people and promoting individual human dignity has been a challenge. Consequently, insecurity and instability still persist in these societies in the post-conflict period.

Strong ethnic ties[21] and limited resources[22] in Africa have the tendency to constrain the political will of leaders to practically embark on a broad-based nationalistic agenda. Economic opportunities are constantly channeled toward particular ethnic groups and some privileged few. Though this is counter-productive, the phenomenon is well entrenched in post-conflict states. The result has been an extremely slow post-conflict recovery and fragile political stability contrary to the overarching goal of achieving political stability, economic recovery, and human well-being in the post-conflict era. In some cases, the strategy has been to appease the rebels or political opponents through the offering of positions in the government.[23] Some have noted this as a form of power-sharing arrangement.[24] In the Sierra Leonean case, for instance, the Lome and the Abidjan Peace Accords devoted most of their provisions to appeasing the RUF by offering a high-level political position to the rebel leader, Forday Sankoh, and comfortably resettling the rebels and former combatants. Nothing in the peace agreement specifically addressed the situation of innocent war victims[25] and how to compensate and restore them to dignified lives. This created a "lose-lose" situation for the victims, some of whom lost limbs; they face a bleak and challenging future. In a *National Geographic* documentary on the Sierra Leonean civil war titled "Blood Money," many of the war victims complained bitterly about being neglected by the government, and that the resettlement of former rebel combatants has been the government's priority instead. They question the wisdom in them not taking part in the war since it would have put them in a more favorable situation just as the rebels are enjoying after the conflict.

Post-war peace-building and recovery strategies need to be examined and the shortcomings addressed. This book broadly examines conflict management strategies and post-conflict recovery in Sierra Leone as the country makes an effort at peace consolidation and transition to economic recovery and development. Importantly, it is the goal of this book to examine the extent to which human security issues that are critical to after-conflict peace consolidation and economic recovery have been addressed and subsequently implemented in the post-conflict reconstruction process in Sierra Leone. Post-conflict recovery is about the people and the institutions that promote their safety and well-being.

THE SIERRA LEONEAN SITUATION

Understanding the Sierra Leonean civil war is critical to the post-conflict strategies to stabilize the country and put it on the path to development. Security in Sierra Leone can open the country to investment opportunities not only from foreigners but also the Sierra Leonean diaspora. Understanding the nature of the war could also avoid wasting resources on strategies that do not deal with the core of the conflict which usually is a one-size-fits-all approach to resolving conflict in Africa.

The Sierra Leone Civil War

Sierra Leone's civil war has been analyzed from several perspectives; the analysis highlights the dynamism associated with specific conflict situations, and most importantly, understanding the root cause of the conflict. The analyses also indicate how complex civil war situations are, and how any attempt to prescribe a wholesale solution is flawed.

Proponents of spill-over effects of war have largely argued that a conflict in a contiguous state is likely to destabilize other states in the region. Subsequently, the civil war in Liberia has been one of the reasons why the Sierra Leonean war occurred.[26] The Liberian civil war that started in 1989 spilled over to Sierra Leone when Charles Taylor,[27] then president of Liberia, offered to support Forday Sankoh's RUF to destabilize Sierra Leone. It is also noted that Charles Taylor's support for RUF's cause was to punish Sierra Leone for the country's role in the peace-keeping mission in Liberia. In spite of these narratives, there is overwhelming evidence in the literature that the onset of the war in Sierra Leone is better explained by the irresponsible behaviors of the country's political elites who pursued parochial and self-centered policies in post-independent Sierra Leone. These behaviors have weakened the society, its economy, and, broadly, the development of the country.

Sierra Leone's political elites have continually betrayed the power and trust the Sierra Leonean people placed in them to manage the country's politics and economy. They are faulted in engaging in unethical practices leading to favoritism and corruption. These practices invariably resulted in a weak central government, and created in and out group entities which led to the exclusion of some part of the Sierra Leonean population and created tensions—a recipe for potential violence.[28] Corruption leads to apathy on the part of political elites in governing a state; it also impacts negatively on its institutions and people. States where corruption is notoriously entrenched, leaders have lost political authority.[29] Consequently, and without elites noticing, a power "vacuum" is created and filled by lawless individuals who may also be influential members of the society. Thus, although there are political leaders in control of the state and directing affairs, there also exist other parallel political structures. Sierra Leone's politics is described as "warlordization" to describe the consequences of poor governance and weak government[30] arising out of corruption. Leaders such as Siaka Stevens were able to survive in Sierra Leone because they relied on a loyal paramilitary capable of intimidating any potential rivals. The act of corruption reveals the shortsightedness of elites regarding the political future of a country. It also disregards institutions, the lack of trust in such institutions, and the stability and development of the state.

Again, Sierra Leone's civil war has been encapsulated "in the recklessness with which its political elites have callously undermined the hopes and aspirations of its people for political stability and the sustained improvement of living standards."[31] For most of the period after independence, Sierra Leone's elites have continually exploited the already volatile relationship that existed between the various ethnic groups in Sierra Leone. Like a divide and rule strategy, the elite exploited vulnerable groups to hold on to political power. The inherited structures of an ethnically balkanized state like Sierra Leone provide political elites the opportunities to exploit the situation to further fractionalize the population by transforming ethnicity into class.[32]

Much of the tension that culminated in the civil war could also be attributed to a systematic behavior, overtly or covertly, of political elites' blatant exclusion of segments of the Sierra Leonean population.[33] This reduces the capacity of the excluded groups to make legitimate political demands on the government. When such a situation occurs, the only prudent option left for the marginalized group to overcome this odd is to pick up arms and overthrow the government. This group could also become potential recruits for rebel leaders and other social and political opportunists.

Like the Arab Spring that swept through North Africa and other parts of the Middle East, the Sierra Leone civil conflict was seen as a revolutionary war to change the status quo. However, lawless individuals such as Forday Sankoh and Charles Taylor hijacked the revolutionary war to further their own political interests.[34] The revolutionary war was traced to the 1970s and 1980s as a result of the government's lack of concern for the youth in Sierra Leone which resulted in a "ghetto mentality" around the time,[35] and the youth's search for opportunities to reverse the political and economic disequilibrium.[36] However, the revolution that the student movement had planned disintegrated because of a disagreement between the student leaders; Forday Sankoh took advantage of the situation to further his own dubious political agenda.[37]

The battle for the control of strategic economic resources has plagued many post-independent states in Africa. This has resulted in the destruction of the social, political, and economic development of many of those states. Instead of the strategic resources spearheading development and enhancing the well-being of the people, a situation of "resource curse" has occurred leaving the people in misery. The rich diamond deposits (infamously called "blood diamonds") in Sierra Leone have been blamed for the conflict in the country. One of the challenges of managing natural resources in Africa has been how political leaders could position themselves to secure the trust of the people as they manage those state resources. In fact, one of the major challenges to democracy in Sierra Leone continues to be its diamond deposits that have attracted cross-border instability in the country.[38] Hirsch, a former US ambassador to Sierra Leone, was not the only person to make this observation. A Canadian non-governmental organization, Partnership Africa Canada, had also contended that diamonds have been at the heart of political instability in Sierra Leone since it was discovered in the 1930s. Enclave economy crowds out the economic opportunity field within the state since most, if not all, of the development resources are channeled toward a specific venture to the neglect of other potential ventures within the state. Political leaders effectively cease to institute policies that expand the economy since the status quo benefits them.

Thus thorough analysis of the literature on the civil conflict in Sierra Leone reveals the lack of political will on the part of political elites to positively develop institutions and state structures to harness all the human and material resources of the state. Exclusion resulting from greed and the lack of vision on the part of the leadership has been the bedrock of the conflict in Sierra Leone in particular, and a repeated cause of most conflicts in Africa. The blatant neglect and irresponsible behavior of political elites to disregard a huge segment of the population is troubling. It is important to note that both minority and majority (South Africa during the Apartheid regime) groups could be victims of marginalization. Marginalization in these societies is carefully planned strategies and there are institutions (visible or invisible) to support such acts. However, once a group is threatened by neglect, exclusion, or marginalization, they have always found a way to fight back in the attempt to change the status quo.

MANAGING THE POST-CONFLICT ERA

Two fundamental political arrangements implemented in the post-conflict to manage the after-conflict era have been to organize an election to establish a democratic system. This is sometimes supplemented with a power-sharing arrangement. Establishing a democratic system is to rectify some of the institutional weaknesses within the states. People get to know beforehand what the rules are and the dynamics of engaging the governing system. Transparency is assured in a system of democracy. However, there are no guarantees regarding how such a system will respond to the needs of the people. It should be noted that most of these states that underwent violent conflicts had leaders who were elected through organized elections. Examples are Liberia, Sierra Leone, Cote D'Ivoire, Mozambique, Kenya, and Zimbabwe. If this is the case, then positively coordinated system/people dynamic becomes critical in the post-conflict. We are talking about how such institutions established in the post-conflict help provide opportunities and restore people's dignity—human security.

Democratic Transitions and the Post-Conflict Era

Though establishing a democratic process and creating democratic institutions could provide a respite for states emerging from violent conflicts, the short-term challenges of the process impact the long-term benefits. The democratization process in Africa poses serious challenges to many societies that want to transition, and even more precarious for those emerging from violent conflict. The unintended consequence for many of them is increased domestic tension and, in some cases, full-blown conflict. In analyzing fourteen major peace-building missions conducted between 1989 and 1999, Paris[39] argued that, though there is sound wisdom in the transformation of conflict-ridden states into market democracies,[40] pushing this process too fast could have some damaging, destabilizing, and unintended consequences including the undermining of the prospects for sustainable peace. In most cases post-conflict states are exposed to "stabilizing" strategies that are incompatible with each other. Clear distinction must be made between post-conflict reconstruction and normal development. In the post-conflict, trust in the governing system is critical. People need to be assured that government can be relied upon for their safety and well-being. Strong domestic institutions, which have the capability of creating a strong foundation for the democratic process, must first be pursued.

Semi-democracies[41] are more likely to experience civil conflict.[42] Semi-democracies are partly open societies; however, they still possess repressive state apparatus. This combination is a good opportunity for the organization of protests, rebellion, and other forms of violent conflicts. Government attempts to quell such protest could lead to a full-blown conflict due to the lack of appropriate protest-managing resources. Repression leads to grievances that encourage groups to take action; the openness of the society, in terms of some freedom of expression and association, enables these groups to organize themselves in certain activities against the government.[43] In some African communities, such freedoms of speech and expression have led to extreme disrespect for those in authority. Situations like these are expected, especially when such freedoms have been denied for a very long time and the people are faced with the dilemma of whether to internalize their grievances as before, or how to use such freedoms. On the other hand, authorities are used to being accorded the utmost respect for their leadership and find it unbearable to cope with a situation where insults and other acts of disrespect are directed against them. In Africa, there are unwritten laws and those that engage in insults against state leaders are punished accordingly, through police or paramilitary harassments. Again, states going through democratic transitions encounter serious internal instability at least in the initial stages, making them politically unstable.[44]

Liberal democracy introduces a new mechanism regarding how benefits are to be distributed. Thus, those who previously received preferential benefits will feel threatened that the new political system may dispossess them of their previous privileges and entitlements. A contemporary case is the reconsideration of the de-Baathification[45] policy in Iraq after Saddam Hussein's government was overthrown in 2003. It was noted, at least by some policymakers, that part of the explanation to the protracted violence in Iraq could be attributed to resentment from those who previously had benefited from the Hussein government (mainly the Sunni bloc) and were excluded from the sharing of certain privileges in the post-Saddam Hussein era. Incidence of civil violence in India ironically stemmed from the establishment of India's democratic institutions.[46] Increased access of technology, education, grassroots political power, and unbounded power of the media, ushered in social change leading to those categorized as untouchables and other underprivileged people changing their social strata within the society. There were also various accusations by religious groups (Hindus and Muslims) about which of them was gaining ground in Indian society, all as a result of the inception of the democratization process.[47] Such short-term challenges of the democratization process require a strong political will on the part of government to continue the course of political openness and good governance. However, some leaders are either overwhelmed or scared that the initial reaction to the new reality could plunge the state to instability and therefore resort to oppressive strategies and tactics that could invariably become institutionalized.

Political elites rely on a certain core group of the population to help them win and stay in power. This group is usually referred to as the minimum winning coalition. Political elites, like business entrepreneurs, would like to minimize electoral costs and maximize their vote share and power. Thus, they are more concerned about that core group of people who help them to win elections and to consolidate their power. In dictatorships, it is the military and few high level cronies that really matter to the leadership. Since dictators have only a small number of people they rely on to hold on to power, they are more inclined to provide private goods.[48] A change to a democratic system, on the other hand, tips the scale toward having to rely on a majority of the population. Leaders, thus, need the support of a majority of the population to acquire and maintain power.[49] Thus, political elites and governments in democracies, out of necessity would provide public goods.[50]

However, in ethnically divided societies, those that the elite rely on to hold onto power are those that belong to their respective ethnic groups and other close acquaintances. Consequently, though the public goods would be provided, it would be targeted to a particular ethnic group.

Political ideologies play a role in the governing process. It is a guide that directs political parties and elites regarding the values that need to be maintained within the society and the role of government in achieving these values. Such values also have implications for the level of development. However, political ideologies in Africa are not so much about what the politicians profess them to be, but rather who they truly identify with regards to what ethnic group they emanate from.[51] Such ideologies effectively elevate the values of one ethnic group above the others and further create tensions.

Cultural polarization may result from the democratization process. In some instances in Africa, this has become the rule instead of an exception, where it becomes apparent that ethnic groups cannot rely on the central government for protection; the consequent security dilemma creates an incentive for the emergence of group-level mobilization.[52] This situation is a recipe for the onset of internal conflict.

Political instability has become one of the unintended consequences of the democratic process in Africa. Many of the states have evolved into fragile/weak democracies. There seems to be a positive relationship between democracy and the emergence of civil conflict in some states contrary to the peace and stability[53] witnessed in advanced democratic states. It is evident in findings in post-colonial Africa that there is no positive relationship between democracy and internal stability across all societies. The implication suggests that a democratic process does not necessarily reduce the incidence of internal conflict. Democratic enlargement is not a recipe for peace, and, thus, to use it as a strategy for resolving conflict is not likely to lead to the intended outcome.[54] The above arguments do not necessarily suggest that democratic processes and transitions lack essence when applied in the post-conflict. What they imply is the responsiveness of such a system to the needs of the people. The extent to which the system is trusted and creates opportunities for the people becomes imperative in the post-conflict.

Power Sharing and Conflict Management

An approach used by stakeholders to augment the weakness in the electoral process,[55] and to ensure peace, equity, stability, and development is a power-sharing government. Examples are the power-sharing governments in Kenya, Zimbabwe, Cote D'Ivoire,[56] and South Sudan.[57] Power-sharing comes in many forms. In Burundi, for instance, a form of power-sharing arrangement has been set up to guarantee both Hutus and Tutsis a certain percentage of the senate, the military, and the cabinet. The Twa, the other minority groups, have also been guaranteed some extra seats in Parliament.

Power-sharing, as a strategy for conflict resolution, has its own shortcomings. This includes the tendency to breed insecurity and a high level of distrust on all sides. Any policy recommendation by parties is considered as giving that party an advantage and this may threaten the other party or parties. There is the tendency for parties not to have enough room to actively engage the political, economic, and societal issues that confront the state as a result of such suspicions. The result has been governing stalemate as the Kenyan and Zimbabwean cases made clear. There also appears to be a situation where parties have to overly defend policy stance which leads to divisive government. The belligerents, now forced to form governing coalition, do not trust the commitment they have agreed to. Power-sharing deals become an opportunity to get close to each other and possibly discredit the "political enemy" by vehemently vilifying the opponent of any policy suggestion. Among the critical reasons why power-sharing agreements have failed is that they create governing regimes without addressing fundamental issues in the society.[58]

The lack of effective institutions has plagued most African states, making them politically unstable. Workable institutions that enhance the well-being of the people are therefore necessary for political stability. Power-sharing, as a strategy, leads to the institutionalization of "internal factionalism, divisions, and politics that afflict all ethnic communities."[59] Closely related to this institutionalization of ethnic fractionalization is that power-sharing tends to perpetuate inter-communal conflict by the institutionalization of differences at the highest political level, which also encourages extremism.[60]

An unproductive approach to any post-conflict peace strategy is creating ethnic consciousness within the polity. Power-sharing provides the opportunity for political elites to make all issues ethnic issues. These political elites usually seek ethnic issues that tend to strengthen the support among their own ethnic groups.[61] The use of power-sharing as a conflict management strategy, therefore, is likely to lead to the institutionalization and escalation of ethnic tensions.

Power-sharing is a temporary stop-gap strategy for reducing tensions. In the long run, the weaknesses, as noted above, do not help to ensure sustainable peace critically needed for successful post-conflict reconstruction and development. Power-sharing effectively eliminates the productive party-in-opposition necessary for checking and balancing the ruling government and institutions—a critical foundation of the democratic process.

In the developing world such as Africa, where resources are limited and political power tends to have a positive correlation with economic power,[62] power-sharing governments widen the "plundering agents" of the country's resources, with no strong opposition party to serve as a check on the government. The chances for the people to share in the decision-making process are limited and so is the people's ability to share in the nation's resources.

In power-sharing governments, more time is spent on accusations and counter-accusations within the government itself, leaving less time for actual developmental discussions to take place. In Kenya and Zimbabwe, it took a long time for the cabinet positions to be allocated between the president and the prime minister's office. Ongoing discussions were still on the table regarding what roles each of the parties will be responsible for till the 2012 elections eliminated the power-sharing governments in both countries. The situation is made more complex due to the different ideologies and approaches to government by the respective power-sharing partners. In Cote D'Ivoire, Laurent Gbagbo dissolved a power-sharing government over electoral process dispute in 2010. This led to an eventual civil war and Gbagbo's arrest in April of 2011 by forces loyal to Allassane Ouattara.

The Paradox of the Post-Conflict

Post-conflict reconstruction presents a dilemma for policy-makers and other stakeholders who want to find ways to ensure stable post-conflict political, social, and economic environment after violent domestic conflicts. In Africa, the objective and the process appear to run parallel and this leads to slower after-conflict recovery. The objective has been to ensure stability and security. The process, however, faces numerous challenges, including what kind of institutions to put in place and whether or not to adopt institutions that are foreign or to develop institutions domestically from the ground up. The one other important question with regard to what exactly is to be reconstructed could better be described as a paradox. The World Bank's initial effort to assist states emerging from violent conflicts was to rebuild ruined physical infrastructure necessary for the productivity and employment. The strategy looked promising. However, fixing these physical structures did not lead to expected development and improved living standards for the people. The Bank's Post-Conflict Fund (PCF) established in August 1997 was to support states in transition from conflict to sustainable peace. Most of these funds went into demobilization, disarmament, and reintegration (DDR) of ex-combatants. In the case of Albania, for instance, the PCF was used mainly to expand infrastructure facilities needed by refugees. This is basically prolonging temporariness[63] which is the reality in dealing with the refugee situations across the globe, including Dadaab in Kenya.

In the aftermath of World War II, the Marshall Plan, though a strategy to contain the expansive influence of the Soviet Union on the rest of Europe, was very effective when the United States injected a massive amount of finance capital to help Western Europe rebuild from the ruins of the devastating war, and to place their economies on the path to enhanced development.

This effort was very successful because Western Europe, before World War II, was already developed with well-established and coordinated institutions that supported the existing productive infrastructure. Thus, the fund assistance by the Breton Woods institutions[64] was effectively put to good use. Massive infrastructure build-up and the structuring of the economies of Western European states, backed by already established coordinated institutions, enabled quick recovery in the reconstruction and development of these states.

African states however, were not bequeathed effective and well-coordinated institutions at independence. A striking permanent (politico-socio-economic) institution that independent Africa inherited from colonialism was the linkage of the respective economies to that of the colonial masters, making Africa permanent supplier of primary goods to feed industries in the Western world. This relationship accounts, in part, for underdevelopment of most African states because the advanced world continues to siphon the surplus resources that are produced by the developing world.[65] Post-independent African leaders, interestingly, did not make the development of effective institutions a priority when given the opportunity. This missed opportunity ensured that political elites did not create or establish effective and coordinated institutions necessary for political, civil, economic, and personal securities to strengthen their respective societies and put them on the path to development. Leaders at independence followed the status quo and further oppressed their fellow people whom they struggled with for independence. Most of these states became "Frankenstein" states where political leaders threatened and held their own people hostage from their liberties, resulting in mass poverty, internal tensions, and conflicts.[66] The lack of effective and sustainable institutions did not just threatened citizens of these conflict states, it also affected the entire security of the region.[67]

In the post-conflict era, especially in Africa, the challenge becomes what exactly African leaders and other stakeholders are to reconstruct after the violent internal conflicts. Efforts at achieving a peaceful post-conflict era, however, have shuttled between "what should be"[68] and "what should have been"[69] strategies. As the World Bank's initial experience indicates, what had been the primary concern was to rebuild ruined infrastructure. Though this effort is not necessarily a bad idea, it does not address the fundamental issues that make these states unstable in the first place, and which invariably led to the conflict. In the case of Sierra Leone the policy decisions and attitudes of political elites are fundamental to the instability which finally imploded into the eleven-year civil conflict. Thus building physical infrastructures in the post-conflict is effectively the superimposition of needed structures on faulty or fragile institutional foundations—a "what should be" strategy. On the other hand, most of these states that go through violent domestic conflicts lack fundamental institutional and state capacities that make them weak and unable to control their respective territorial sovereignty and integrity. Citizens' daily lives are threatened by deliberately structured marginalization policies on the part of the political elites to consciously target the exclusion of a majority or specific section of the population, and to close all areas of opportunities available to these people. The post-conflict requires comprehensive analysis of the conflict situation. The "what should have been" strategy that establishes fundamental political, economic, and social institutions is critical and meaningful to citizens both in peace time and after-conflict situations. In the after-conflict, "what should have been" strategies establish the rules of fairness and secured guarantees for which essential physical infrastructure becomes relevant and a key part of the recovery process.

POST-CONFLICT RECONSTRUCTION IN THE AFRICAN SETTING

Post-conflict reconstruction framework in Africa has involved the implementation of ad-hoc strategies aimed at achieving a seemingly peaceful and sustainable after-conflict environment. These strategies must carefully be planned and specifically tailored against the backdrop that more than 50 percent of countries that have been in conflict have actually gone back to the battleground again or are fragile and at risk of sliding back into conflict. "The sustainable reconstruction of countries emerging from long periods of conflict is a challenge we ignore at our own peril. This is not an issue we can relegate to the sidelines of development."[70] The World Bank's initial involvement in post-conflict reconstruction in Africa was centered on the "reconstruction" of ruined infrastructure in African states. This framework was fashioned alongside the 1940s strategy used in Europe to reconstruct ruined infrastructure necessary to jump-start the industrialization efforts of these Western European states. Obviously, this strategy is flawed since most of these states that are experiencing or have experienced violent domestic conflicts do not even have the appropriate institutions to support these infrastructures for any meaningful development. The World Bank, however, has recognized this flaw and redirected its post-conflict reconstruction efforts to include the establishment and strengthening of social, political, and economic institutions in these post-conflict states in order to steer these states on the course to sustainable peace and development.[71]

As states emerge from violent internal conflict, their nature and other core structures may be fundamentally altered. Some of these states could emerge from the conflict with new political elites in power such as Libya, Rwanda, Cote D'Ivoire, and Kenya. The population dynamics at the end of the conflict may not be as they had existed before. For instance, certain ethnic groups that were in the minority could become influential and strong power brokers as in the case of Rwanda. In prolonged conflicts, rebels from other neighboring states that have come to fight in the war could make the new state their home. Examples could be the Tuaregs and other foreign Islamists that made Northern Mali their new home after the war that toppled the government of Muammar Gadhafi. Other issues may include the state of the existing functioning institutions[72] that need to be salvaged as strategies are formulated to deal with the after-conflict reconstruction and recovery. When a change in control of government occurs after the post-conflict, then we should expect power consolidation to be a priority on the to-do list of the new political elite. They may be preoccupied with activities and policies to gain the trust of the people and may want to walk this balance very well. Secondly, expectations become uncertain when, for instance, the new regime embarks on ambitious programs that alter existing societal structures and government like we currently have in Egypt.[73] The situation becomes even precarious when effective institutions are non-existent. When the Hussein government in Iraq was deposed, the political, legal, as well as the cultural dynamics of Iraq changed and that accounts for the daunting task the state faced in the post-conflict.[74]

An all-encompassing or comprehensive strategy is necessary for the success of post-conflict reconstruction, especially with regard to security issues.[75] Security governance is an effective measure for dealing with post-war security challenges because war-torn states lack the capacity to manage the post-conflict. Also, because the threats to security in the post-conflict are multilayered, multifaceted, and interconnected, a holistic approach is needed; this should involve external and internal actors such as non-state armed actors and even war lords,[76] some of whom may be citizens genuinely looking for opportunities to a dignified life. Because non-state actors have become relevant, external and government forces should not ignore but engage and collaborate with them in achieving a successful post-conflict stability.

An all-encompassing strategy, though slow and tedious, appears to be a prudent approach in post-conflict situations. Prominent African leaders have also argued that various constituents of the society need to be part of any post-conflict reconstruction efforts.[77] In addressing the management of African conflict, Salim Ahmed Salim[78] calls for an integrated overall approach in resolving conflict. This approach involves the ingenuity of political leaders, civil society, intellectuals, and students engaging each other in a positive atmosphere during the post-conflict era as they craft strategies to put the country back on the road to security and development. In the Sierra Leonean case, the youth question[79] became the centerpiece of any meaningful discussion. The energy of the youth is a double-edged sword. It could be a tremendous asset but could also be a burden if not managed properly in the post-conflict era.

Equity also becomes a critical element in the post-conflict. This is an important signal that an old era of discrimination and exclusion is over and a new era of acceptance and relevance is ushered in. Peace and reconstruction need to be founded on the premise of equality among the various constituents of the society. Injecting gender[80] sensitivities into the post-conflict discourse, by explicitly making equality between the sexes a fundamental issue is critical if the goal of achieving sustainable peace in the post-conflict is to be achieved.[81] The era when men are the only actors on the battlefield is over. Contemporary conflicts are fought on urban and rural streets with women participating as soldiers or rebels. In most cases they also become victims of the war when they are raped, brutalized, or placed in inhumane servitude roles. Thus women are more susceptible to security threats than men. Women are the ones mostly affected by poverty, displacement, hunger, and disease as a result of the war.[82]

The ultimate expectation in the post-conflict era is the creation of an enabling environment where established institutions guarantee security and freedoms necessary for development. The current US strategy regarding post-conflict reconstruction is to assist such states to build some minimum level of capacity to help sustain the fragile peace realized in the post-conflict.[83] This involves the creation of enabling conditions and other institutions that were previously weak or non-existent in the pre-conflict period. Critical among these conditions are security, governance and participation, social and economic well-being, and justice and reconciliation. The success of post-conflict reconstruction needs to be anchored in a comprehensive strategy in terms of creating effective institutions within a society-specific environment to support post-conflict peace and development.

As social constructivist will note, the state is a social construct that constantly changes. The ease of movement within contemporary globalized environment and advancement in communication technology necessitate a critical view of the post-conflict state. Gathering information, other materials, and financial resources to achieve a successful post-conflict reconstruction is laborious and challenging. This, however, is the essence of the post-conflict. The alternative of either to do nothing or to put in place a hurriedly organized strategy is not a prudent option, especially when global security is at a tipping point and extremists are looking for unstable states as safe havens.

IMPORTANCE AND ORGANIZATION OF THE BOOK

Though this book provides an alternative for thinking about prudent strategies needed in the post-conflict era, it is also relevant for strengthening fragile states. The discussion so far has placed human security (discussed in chapter 2) at the center of any post-conflict reconstruction effort. The discussions mainly focused on analyzing conflict and the conflict situation in Sierra Leone. However, examples were drawn from the rest of Africa to help put the Sierra Leonean situation in a broader African perspective. The book also draws attention to the fact that conflict starts with people and ends with people. It puts forth the concept of human security as an alternative strategy in achieving sustainable peace in the after-conflict. The book views human security as an independent variable. Human security, unlike national security, is not easily obtained even when policies are established to achieve that target. Human security is a double-edged sword. It could be a challenge to the status quo especially when leaders are not sure they have consolidated power to ensure their political survival. In that case, it is a disincentive to the political elites whose responsibility it is to ensure human security. On the other hand, with appropriate and effective institutions, human security can enhance peace, stability, and development, which can help elites to hold on to power at less cost. This book views human security in the second perspective and that it is being seen as a driving force in the post-conflict recovery process. For states emerging from violent conflict, human security is a critical element for sustainable peace and recovery in the post-conflict era. The lack of it leads to fragile peace, instability, and slower recovery.

The conflict puzzle has three significant components: the cause(s) of the conflict, strategies to resolve the conflict, and commitment to sustainable post-conflict peace-building. The strategy to resolve the conflict, which includes the signing of peace agreements, is a significant component of the conflict puzzle. Not only does it constitute a framework toward sustainable post-conflict reconstruction efforts, it also assists in ameliorating, if not eliminating potential future conflicts. The strategy to resolve the conflict also includes the people and both the short- and long-term efforts to improve their lives. Since 1967, Sierra Leone has not been able to successfully manage domestic stability. Successive political leaders have adopted policies that clearly favored one group over the other(s). Entrenched fragile domestic situations thus developed since the 1967 elections until 2002 when the conflict was officially declared ended. There are no alternatives to establishing appropriate institutions that create stability. When those institutions are not established in the first place, the resulting effect will be the superimposition of post-conflict reconstruction and recovery efforts on existing fragile domestic conditions. The book argues for human security to be made part of the post-conflict reconstruction process by establishing appropriate reforms and other institutions.

This book also serves as a policy tool for conflict management. It prompts policymakers and other stakeholders interested in conflict management to rethink existing conflict management strategies. The security dilemma that results in arms races in international politics is at play and underlies the spate of civil conflicts in Africa. As some secure political power, and enrich themselves economically, the life and security of the majority of the people who do not have such access are threatened. The work therefore proposes a human security approach to conflict management to guide future conflict resolution strategies in Africa and elsewhere. As scholars have argued, the security discourse has shifted from focusing on national security to human security which seeks to reduce internal tension and to promote development.[84]

The book is organized into six chapters. Chapter 1—introduction—explored the issue of development in security. It analyzed how security and stability are critical to the efforts at achieving expected targets during the post-conflict era. The first few years of the post-conflict are critical and the understanding of the conflict, the societal realities, and relevant institutions become a priority. Thus, chapter 1 reviewed the literature on Sierra Leonean's civil conflict. It also discusses the unintended consequences of the democratic process (including power-sharing) in states in transition. The chapter also analyzes the post-conflict reconstruction process and highlights certain critical steps. Chapter 2 examines the human security concept alongside other strategies for dealing with marginalization and exclusions. It argues that the nature of the human security concept should serve as an incentive for policymakers, to make it a priority, since it is the hub for post-conflict stability and development. Chapter 3 examines the political and civil reforms in Sierra Leone. It analyzes the Local Government Act of 2004 which happens to be one of the prominent political documents in post-conflict Sierra Leone. The chapter also examines issues of rule of law and other civil rights and liberty imperatives. Chapter 4 addresses economic reforms in post-conflict Sierra Leone. It discusses efforts at various levels to ensure economic security and development which includes social and economic safety nets. The youth question is also analyzed to address the increased youth unemployment problem. Chapter 5 discusses personal security reforms. It examines national, provincial, district, and local strategies to enforce security in the country. Chapter 6 looks at human security in post-conflict Sierra Leone. Making the argument that human security is the bedrock of successful post-conflict reconstruction in Sierra Leone, the chapter analyzes the current reforms within the context of a human security framework. Chapter 6 concludes with some policy suggestions for sustainable peace and development in post-conflict Sierra Leone.

NOTES

1. Though the term refers to tools and policies that originally target and stabilize states that are emerging out of violent conflicts, such policies are also applied in states that are considered fragile and have a potential to slide into violent conflict.

2. This book deals with post-conflict reconstruction in Sierra Leone. In order not to confuse readers regarding issues of levels of analysis, when the book mentions Africa, the statement or argument is also applicable to Sierra Leone.

3. See a discussion by Ben K. Fred-Mensah, "Social Capital Building as Capacity for Postconflict Development: The UNDP in Mozambique and Rwanda," *Global Governance*: 10 (2004), 437–57.

4. See Thomas Hobbes. *Leviathan*. New York: Oxford University Press, 1996.

5. See John Locke. *Two Treatises of Government: A Classical Work of Philosophy*. Anonymously published in 1689.

6. See Ali Mazrui. "The Frankenstein State and the International Order," in Laremont, Rene Ricardo, and Fouad Kalouche (eds.) *Africa and Other Civilizations: Conquest and Conquest-Conquest*. Trenton, NJ: Africa World Press, Inc., 2002.

7. A political merger was accomplished in the Protectorate when several entities including the Sierra Leone Organization Society, Protectorate Educational Progressive Union, Peoples Party—cultural nationalist, Lamina Sankoh, and moderate Krio formed the Sierra Leone Peoples Party led by the first medical doctor of the Protectorate, Dr. Milton Margai.

8. See Earl Conteh-Morgan and Mac Dixon-Fyle. 1999. *Sierra Leone at the End of the Twentieth Century: History, Politics, and Society*. New York: Peter Lang Publishing, Inc.

9. By choice or sheer ignorance, some political elites have discounted the invaluable potentials of their own people. Promoting and protecting the citizenry have not been a policy priority.

10. Political stability is imperative. Every leader recognizes that. However, achieving stability when conflict had already taken off is tricky and sometimes too late. Since it is the people that oftentimes rise to challenge the government, the strategy for political stabilization should focus on the people.

11. See D. L. Horowitz. 1985. *Ethnic Groups in Conflict*. Berkeley: University of California Press; A. Wimmer, et al. 2004. *Facing Ethnic Conflicts: Toward a New Realism*. Lanham, MD: Rowman & Littlefield Publishers, Inc.

12. See R. Ganguly and R. C. Taras. 1998. *Understanding Ethnic Conflict: The International Dimension*. New York: Addison-Wiley Educational Publishers Inc., p. 20.

13. Ibid.

14. See Paul Collier and Anke Hoeffler. 2000. *Greed and Grievance in Civil Wars*. Washington, DC: World Bank Development Research Group.

15. See Mats Berdal and David M. Malone (eds.) 2000. *Greed and Grievance: Economic Agendas in Civil Wars*. Boulder, CO: Lynne Reinner Publishers, Inc., p. 5.

16. See Musifiky Mwanasali. 2000. "The View from Below," in Mats Berdal and David M. Malone (eds.) *Greed and Grievance: Economic Agendas in Civil Wars* . Boulder, CO: Lynne Reinner Publishers, Inc., p. 140.

17. See Rene Lemarchand. 1995. *Burundi: Ethnic conflict and Genocide*. New York: Wilson Center Press.

18. See Barbara Harff and Ted Gurr. 1994. *Ethnic Conflict in World Politics*. Boulder, CO: Westview Press.

19. See Kendra Dupuy and Helga Malmin Binningsbo. 2007. *Power-sharing and Peacebuilding in Sierra Leone: Power-Sharing Agreements, Negotiations, and Peace Process*. CSCW papers, Center for the Study of Civil War, PRIO.

20. Human security is human-centered security. The idea that resources and institutions should focus on making the human-being secured in his/her own person in order to live a dignified life.

21. See D.L. Horowitz. 1985. *Ethnic Groups in Conflict*. Berkeley: University of California Press.

22. See Paul Collier, Anke Hoeffler, and Dominic Rohner. "Beyond Greed and Grievance: Feasibility and Civil War." *Center for the Study of African Economies,* Working Paper. 10 (7) August, 2006.

23. This is not necessarily a bad idea since in the short term it tends to calm down the tense level of insecurity. On the other hand, the underlying objective of addressing the situation of weal institutions is given less attention.

24. See Kendra Dupuy and Helga Malmin Binningsbo. 2007. *Power-sharing and Peacebuilding in Sierra Leone: Power-Sharing Agreements, Negotiations, and Peace Process*. CSCW papers, Center for the Study of Civil War, PRIO.

25. These are law-abiding Sierra Leonean people.

26. See Earl Conteh-Morgan and Mac Dixon-Fyle. 1999. *Sierra Leone at the End of the Twentieth Century: History, Politics, and Society*. New York: Peter Lang Publishing, Inc.

27. Charles Taylor was sentenced to fifty years in prison by the Special Courts of Sierra Leone for aiding and abetting as well as planning heinous crimes against humanity in Sierra Leone.

28. This is the general idea contained in Sahr John Kpundeh. 1993. *Elites, Non-Elites and Corruption: An Attitudinal Analysis of Data from Sierra Leone*. PhD Dissertation. Washington, DC: Howard University.

29. See William Reno. 1998. *Warlord Politics and the African State*. Boulder, CO: Lynne Rienner Publishers, Inc.

30. Ibid.

31. See Earl Conteh-Morgan and Mac Dixon-Fyle. 1999. *Sierra Leone at the End of the Twentieth Century: History, Politics, and Society*. New York: Peter Lang Publishing, Inc., p. 1.

32. Ibid.

33. See Jimmy D. Kandeh. "Sierra Leone: Contradictory Class Functionality of the 'Soft' State." *Review of African Political Economy* (1995) 22 (55).

34. See Ibrahim Abdullah. 1997. "Bush Path to Destruction: The Origin and Character of the Revolutionary United Front." *African Development*. 22: 3–4.

35. Ibid.

36. See Ishmael Rashid. 1997. "Subaltern Theory and Youth Crisis." *African Development*. 22: 3–4.

37. Ibid.

38. See John L. Hirsch. 2001. *Sierra Leone: Diamonds and the Struggle for Democracy*. Boulder, CO: Lynne Rienner Publishers, Inc.

39. See Roland Paris. 2004. *At War's End: Building Peace After Civil Conflict*. New York: Cambridge University Press.

40. The objective is to get these states on track to development as quickly as possible so that the people can tap into those economic benefits.

41. These are nations in transition to either being democratic or autocratic

42. See Nils Peter Gleditsch, H. Hegre, Tanja Ellingsen, and Scott Gates. 2001. "Toward a Democratic Civil Peace? Democracy, Political Change and Civil War, 1816-1992." *American Political Science Review* 95 (1): 33–47.

43. Ibid.

44. See James D.Fearon and David D. Laitin. "Ethnicity, Insurgency, and Civil War" *American Political Science Review* 97, 1 (Feb 2003): pp.75–79.

45. De-Baathification was a policy in post-Saddam Hussein Iraq where those associated with the Baath Party of Saddam Hussein were to be removed from all positions of privileges even up to employment in the military and the police. This was done to undo all that Saddam Hussein did and to open a new chapter in Iraq. This policy did not take into consideration the extended networks of the Hussein government for the 24 (1979–2003) years of his rule.

46. See R. Ganguly and R.C. Taras. 1998. *Understanding Ethnic Conflict: The International Dimension*. New York: Addison-Wiley Educational Publishers Inc.

47. Ibid.

48. Private goods have to do with the allocation of specific contracts that are targeted to satisfy cronies of the ruling government.

49. See Bruce Bueno de Mesquita, et al. 2003. *The Logic of Political Survival*. Cambridge, MA: The Massachusetts Institute of Technology Press.

50. Public goods have to do with government providing infrastructure that are not targeted and which benefits the larger population. This involves the construction of roads, schools, creating jobs and the like.

51. See Rene Ricardo Laremont and Fouad Kalouche (eds.). 2002. *Africa and Other Civilizations: Conquest and Conquest-Conquest*. Trenton, NJ: Africa World Press, Inc.

52. See Barry R. Posen. 1993. "The Security Dilemma and Ethnic Conflict." In Michael E. Brown (ed.). *Ethnic Conflict and International Security*. Princeton, NJ: Princeton University Press.

53. See E. A. Henderson. 2002. *Democracy and War: The End of an Illusion?* Boulder, CO: Lynne Rienner Publishers, Inc.

54. Ibid.

55. The electoral process is the fundamental element of the democratic process. However, many political parties and people within states in the developing world have consistently challenge the electoral process and sometimes labeled it illegitimate. In spite of this weakness, there seems to be no legitimate alternative yet to elections and the electoral process.

56. This was put in place in 2003 but had serious problems in 2004 when Gbagbo fired opposition Ministers including the rebel leader Guilaume Soro from his Communications Cabinet position.

57. This was included in the Comprehensive Peace Agreement (CPA) in 2004.

58. See John Harbeson. " Kenya: Power sharing Pacts Have not worked well in Africa." March 31, 2008. Article published on the website of AllAfrica.com

59. See A. Wimmer, et al. 2004. *Facing Ethnic Conflicts: Toward a New Realism*. Lanham, MD: Rowman & Littlefield Publishers, Inc.

60. See I. O'Flynn and Donald Russell (ed.). 2005. *Power-Sharing: Institutional and Social Reform in Divided Societies.* London: Pluto Press. p. 207

61. See P. G. Roeder and Donald Rothchild, (ed.). 2005. *Sustainable Peace: Power and Democracy after Civil Wars*. Ithaca, NY: Cornell University Press.

62. Many have been able to leap-frog the economic ladder just by the mere fact that they are fortunate to be involved in politics at some level.

63. A paradox; IDPs and refugee situations have assumed a permanent nature. Unless stakeholders benefit from this situation, the permanent phenomenon has to stop and displaced people settled quickly to live a dignified life

64. This include the International Bank for Reconstruction and Development (World Bank) and the International Monetary Fund (IMF)

65. See Immanuel Wallerstein. 2004. *World Systems Analysis: An Introduction*. Durham, NC: Duke University press.

66. See Ali Mazrui. 2002. "The Frankenstein State and the International Order." In Laremont, Rene Ricardo, and Fouad Kalouche (eds.). *Africa and Other Civilizations: Conquest and Conquest-Conquest*. Trenton, NJ: Africa World Press, Inc., p. 327

67. See Francis Fukuyama. 2004. *State-building: Governance and World Order in the 21st Century*. Ithaca, NY: Cornell University Press.

68. "What should be" strategies are pre-determined strategies that are imposed on after-conflict African states as a means of securing the peace. This involves procedures such as the organization of elections or some form of broad-based political participation and the re-building of infrastructure and injection of capital.

69. "What should have been" strategies have to do with fundamental political, economic, social, and cultural institutions that need to be present in the first place to ensure a threat-free society.

70. Remarks by James D. Wolfensohn, a former president of the World Bank.

71. See World Bank. 1998. *Post-Conflict Reconstruction: The Role of the World Bank.* Washington, DC: World Bank.

72. Such institutions may include state-wide and tradition institutions.

73. The deposed Morsi government in Egypt was a great concern to Christians and other religious minorities despite statements by the Islamist president that he would be the leader for all Egyptians. Religious-related crimes surged in the early parts of Morsi's regime in Egypt.

74. See Horst Fischer and Noelle Quenivet (eds.). 2005. *Post-Conflict Reconstruction: Nation and/or State-Building.* Berlin: BWV, Berliner Wissenschafts-Verlag.

75. See Alan Bryden and Heiner Hanggi. 2005. *Security Governance in Post-Conflict Peacebuilding*. Piscataway, NJ: Transaction Publishers.

76. See Alan Bryden, Timothy Donais, and Heiner Hanggi. *Shaping Security Governance Agenda in Post-Conflict Peacebuilding.* Geneva: Geneva Center for the democratic Control of Armed Forces, 2005.

77. See Salim Ahmed Salim. 2002. *African Conflicts: Their Management, Resolution and Post-Conflict Reconstruction* Addis Ababa: Development Policy Management Forum.

78. Salim Ahmed Salim was the Secretary General of the OAU (now AU) from September of 1989 to September of 2001.

79. The youth question will be addressed in the subsequent chapters. The term "youth question" has come to be known in Sierra Leone's post-conflict literature as the unacceptable high rate of unemployment among the youth, and the attendant security threats and instability in the post-conflict era.

80. The battlefield has come close to the kitchen, market places, and churches where women are mostly present. Again an equal majority of the population in most societies are women. To post-conflict discussions that ignore their needs is flawed.

81. See Caroline Sweetman. 2005. *Gender, Peace-Building, and Reconstruction*. Oxford: Oxfam.

82. See Ann Tickner. 2004. "Feminist Responses to International Security." *Peace Review* 16 (1): 43–48.

83. See Robert Orr (ed.). *Winning the Peace: An American Strategy for Post Conflict Reconstruction*. Washington, DC: CSIS Press, 2004.

84. See Caroline Thomas and Peter Wilkin (eds.). 1999. *Globalization, Human Security and the African Experience*. Boulder, CO: Lynne Rienner Publishers, Inc.

Chapter Two

Human Security and the Conflict Puzzle

Finding an appropriate theoretical framework to assist in developing appropriate strategies for stability is imperative due to the complex nature of the post-conflict era. Trust, institutional building, and development strategies are all part of the things that need to be done. Our discussions in chapter 1 draw our attention to focus on human development and human-centered strategies if we are to make a positive impact in post conflict.

NAVIGATING THE CONFLICT MANAGEMENT PUZZLE

Attempts at resolving civil conflicts have led to the development of many theories to help provide a better understanding of the causes of conflicts and the effective strategies to curb or resolve them. Some of these conflicts stem from the fact that different ethnicities are unable to tolerate each other. Hence, depluralizing the society could lead to the achievement of ethnic homogeneity by the elimination from the society the non-dominant or "the other" group.[1] The presumption is that ethnically pluralistic societies are inherently unstable and, thus, conflict-prone. By separating the non-dominant group from the dominant group, we have a situation where people within the society would have common customs, interests, and loyalties. However, the notion that depluralizing societies and creating homogeneous ones could lead to political and societal stability is flawed. While it would be extremely difficult to create such a society, there is currently no one single state that could claim perfect societal homogeneity in contemporary times. Even the state widely cited as the perfect homogenous society, Somalia, has been a failed state since 1991 when its elected president, Siad Barre, was ousted from office.

A democratic polity, in principle, has effective tools to manage conflicts. Democratic rules create an informed public and an environment of transparency which ensures an effective process of managing domestic grievances. Leaders in a democratic system occupy political offices as a result of pre-established rules that ensure free choice and fairness.[2] Again, personal grievances could be resolved through appropriate channels established by democratic institutions. In many African states, however, the democratic process has not yielded the intended positive outcomes. The process has not been responsive to the needs of the people. Candidates, who before elections agree that the electoral process is a fair means of electing leaders, quickly question the legitimacy of the process when they lose the election. The consequence has been protests and other civil unrests, and in some cases, violent domestic conflict. Elections in Kenya in December of 2007, the March 2008 and the subsequent run-off elections in June 2008 in Zimbabwe, led to power-sharing governments when the opposition parties rejected the results of the general elections.

Other means of ensuring stability within states have called for political guarantees for minorities or marginalized groups within societies. Notable among these is constitutional engineering that culminates in a consociational system. This strategy is designed to shield marginalized and excluded groups from the oppression of the majority. The consociational system[3] enshrines ownership and control of certain parts of the state to previously marginalized groups. However, what it does not do is to seek those same guarantees for individuals within these fragmented groups in particular, and how the consociational system fits in the overall broad objective of building a stronger state. Thus, the consociational system does not necessarily eliminate marginalization and exclusion within groups; neither does it guarantee cooperating relationship between the leaders of the various groups regarding how to compromise to make the system work[4] and the country strong.

Despite the above conflict management strategies, a significant piece of the conflict management puzzle—how have the people fared after the conflict—is not thoroughly investigated and addressed in the conflict literature. The consociational and the de-pluralizing approaches lead to permanent institutionalization of divided societies.[5] Issues of autonomy within states are complex. In most African states where resources are limited, such policies could lead to secession and weaker state capacities. Even in developed states, the autonomous Basque region and Catalonia in Spain and Quebec in Canada, have continuously threatened secession from the respective states with the Basque region experiencing more violence in the past in the effort to secede. Various ethnicities come to accept the fact that because there are differences among them they have to behave differently resulting in the notion that there are no common grounds for resolving issues.

The electoral democracy[6] approach also suggests that achieving majoritarian rule is a fair basis for resolving conflict. The evidence, however, shows that this has not always been the case.[7] Contemporary conflict management strategies have not taken the root cause of conflict seriously as should have been the case.[8] The result is that the benefit of democratic rules that should trickle down and effectively address the concerns of the people, as expected, is not realized. An important piece of the conflict management puzzle—the people—is sometimes ignored in the after-conflict management process. Conflict management strategies need to embody a trickle-down strategy where guarantees for the safety of the people and enhancing their dignity are assured. Such strategies should be designed to eliminate threats which arise as a result of conscious attempts to stifle the people's rights to participate in the political process, denying civil rights guarantees, the inability to provide employment opportunities, and the fear of personal harm and death are alleviated. It is against this backdrop that the focus on human perspective of conflict resolution is critical in any sustainable conflict management strategy. It transcends other divisionary strategies, and focuses the attention on the people with the goal of creating a safe post-conflict environment that ensures the attainment of self-fulfillment and development.

The rise in internal conflict in most parts of the world has led to unprecedented insecurities in the personal lives of people, increased migration, and poverty. Human security[9] concerns have, therefore, become the critical issue in contemporary security discourse. Haq[10] placed the post–Cold War security environment in the right perspective when he questioned who the real benefactors of security are, as states pursue national security and state interest. Haq noted that countries that pursue national security do so for the security of their own people (i.e., citizens). Thus, the essence of national security is not only to safeguard the territorial integrity of states, but that the resultant stability, peace, and other benefits should trickle down to improve the lives of the people. States develop institutions to achieve domestic order and to enhance the lives of its citizens. The failure to develop institutions that ensure internal security of states has resulted in these states crumbling from within. Referring to the former Soviet Union, Mahbub ul Haq noted that the massive build-up of arms during the Cold War under the cover of boosting national security did not ensure the sustainability of the Union. Poverty, lack of opportunities for individuals to realize their personal dreams, and other insecurities were evident. It was no surprise that when it finally collapsed in 1989 states and people within the Union were far too ready to go their separate ways. Though Haq noted that human security would be achieved through pragmatic developmental strategies that states pursue, it is equally important to note that developmental strategies are unsustainable without human security.

As states in Africa are threatened with a spate of internal conflict, any post-conflict management strategy needs to consider human security as the foundation to sustainable peace and end to conflicts. The youth who enlist as rebels meet two critical life needs: access to guns to ensure their personal security, and wages[11] for their labor, thereby satisfying their economic needs. The youth, therefore, secure their freedom from fear; in this case, they have the guns to protect themselves, and the freedom from want, in which case they receive wages.

In development discourse, a recent paradigm shift has highlighted a human-centered approach to sustainable development. Participatory social learning proponents have argued that development strategies should not be remote to everyday activity and experience of the targeted society.[12] There is therefore a symbiotic relationship between new development concepts and existing development experiences. The two reinforce each other to ensure ownership, innovativeness, and efficiency in development strategies. Making a case for a new economic paradigm of development theory, Wilfred David makes an emphatic plea for a fundamental reorientation, or what he calls a "paradigm shift," from the existing orthodoxy of economic development measures. He calls for "a more participatory conversation of human liberation, or people-centered dialogue, in which human agency becomes the primary unit of interpretation and correlative human choices, capabilities, and freedoms are elevated to center stage of development theory, practice and policy."[13]

Human-centered security in turn creates subsequent securities. The pursuit of wealth by states just for the sake of being wealthy does not necessarily translate to the freedom of its citizens. The wealth of states can be measured not by the value of its gross domestic product (GDP), but rather the freedom its citizens enjoy through the assurances of certain basic societal guarantees within the polity; and that progressive-minded states should create an enabling environment for their citizens to develop their abilities, the failure of which makes development efforts meaningless.[14]

This new wave of development thinking has relevance in strategies necessary for a peaceful and sustainable post-conflict environment. Conflict starts with people and it must end with unequivocally addressing the concerns of the people which was possibly the trigger that started the conflict in the first place. Human beings are rational actors who make choices that bring them more benefits and reduce costs.[15] A conflict management strategy that creates an enabling environment and makes factions foresee a promising "light at the end of the tunnel" is more likely to be sustainable and successful.

An upsurge in internal conflict in the 1990s which neorealist attribute to the end of the Cold War bipolar system,[16] and the genocide in Rwanda in

1994, brought the issue of the security of human beings to the center stage at the UN world body. UNDP dedicated its 1994 human development report to human security, and highlighted the relevance of human security by noting that ensuring "freedom from want" and "freedom from fear" is the effective tool to address contemporary global insecurity. The 1994 Human Development Report, thus, emphasized the need to focus on the individual, and called on governments and international organizations to ensure human security at various levels. The duration of conflict places a heavy burden on people. It is the people who fight, are maimed, and ultimately lose their lives. Most people who join the war as fighters do that to change the status quo with the hope of improving their current deplorable conditions. In Zimbabwe for instance, opposition supporters who had regular and stable jobs ignored a protest called by their party leaders following the deadlock in the 2008 presidential elections.[17] In Nigeria's Niger delta, the people have taken the law into their own hands. They have fought government forces or kidnapped oil company employees for ransom because their economic livelihood and future well-being is threatened.[18] People-centered post-conflict strategy, thus, leads to sustainable after-conflict era.

THE CONCEPT OF HUMAN SECURITY

The concept of human security was pronounced in the 1994 UNDP's Human Development Report (HDR). The concept re-focuses attention to how the international community and domestic policy-makers should view security at the end of the twentieth century and into the twenty-first century. The concept emphasizes human-centered security. This is a paradigmatic shift from the neo-realist concept of security which focuses on the state- national security.

Since the end of World War II the UN and the Security Council have been able to secure world peace leading to the almost eradication of inter-state conflicts. Though states' military budgets continue to rise as they try to protect their territorial integrity and also probably to forestall any threat of terrorism, the security dilemma has not been problematic as in the period before World War II. The liberals may be right in arguing that democracy, interdependence through increased trade, and institutions such as international organizations[19] could bring world peace. As states enjoy peace with each other, some state leaders have used state institutions[20] to oppress their own people. This has resulted in insecurities not only in those states but also the region and the world at large. In these contemporary times when terrorism thrives on pessimism of the future, desperation, and loss of opportunities, the human insecurity concept could not have come at a more opportune time to deal with contemporary security challenges.

The concept of human security is influenced by the promotion of human rights and humanitarian intervention in the post–Cold War era, the upsurge in domestic conflicts, and the decreasing significance of economic indicators for measuring human well-being. Two schools of thought have emerged regarding human security. The narrow school views human security as "the protection of individuals and communities from war and other forms of violence." This is usually referred to as freedom from fear. This conceptual framework of human security seems manageable and has broader appeal since wars and violence are generally rejected.[21] The broad school goes beyond freedom from fear. It also embraces freedom from want. The UNDP human development report (1994) identified seven threats to human security. These include economic security, food security, health security, environmental security, personal security, community security, and political security. An even broader perspective of human security is "to protect the vital core of all human lives in ways that advance human freedoms and human fulfillment."[22] This broad conception of human security has attracted criticism due to it being perceived as having a limitless scope ("vital core of all human lives"). As a result many fear a theory of human security may be intractable.

Aside from the UNDP's efforts at advocating for human security as an ultimate goal for the global society to pursue, some countries have demonstrated intense interest in the emerging concept of human security. Japan has been very instrumental in actually pushing forward the UNDP publication, Human Security Now, in 2003. Japan views human development as pivotal to its human security agenda. The Philippines also passed the Human Security Act of 2007, where an act of terrorism was declared a threat to national security. The Canadian version of human security sided with the UNDP and made the human being the center of the security discourse. The initial 1997 Canadian concept of human security centered on issues such as protecting the rights of children, economic development that focuses on "rules-based trade," disarmament (notably the abolition of anti-personnel landmines), and peacekeeping and peace-building.[23]

Irrespective of how human security is viewed globally, the concept's focus on the well-being of people cannot be overemphasized. The most important resource of a state is its people. The physical, mental, emotional, and psychological health of the people, as well as the availability of opportunities to achieve life goals reflects positively on the strength of the state. This book conceptualizes human security as a means to an end. Thus, human security is seen as an independent variable instead of a dependent variable in the security/development discourse. In this case stability, peace, and development will face enormous challenges in the post-conflict if human security is ignored.

Human Security: Incentives for Political Elites and Governments

Discussions on human security cannot be dissociated from state[24] actions. States have capacities and can use state institutions and structures to develop and safeguard human security. This responsibility is a major challenge to governments in post-conflict states who are tasked with achieving after-conflict stability, peace, and development. The International Commission on Intervention and State Sovereignty (ICISS)[25] and its Responsibility to Protect (R2P) has made a government's responsibility to its citizens even more pronounced. State sovereignty is now considered a privilege not a right. State leaders can request various forms of assistance from the international community if they believe they lack the capacity to ensure an enabling environment for stability to forestall any potential current and future conflicts. Leaders of states that have undergone conflicts in Africa sometimes lack the legitimacy[26] and the capacity to establish institutions critical for human security. Many states in Africa are experiencing severe domestic instability which ranges from a complete collapse (as in the case of Somalia), to weak political system (as observed in DR Congo and South Sudan), intertwined with sorely deep-rooted ethnic coalition that hinders any attempt at human security.[27] Since government efforts are critical in securing human security, appropriate incentives are required to encourage governments to work toward the creation of an enabling environment that ensures such guarantees.

Political elites in charge of governing the state are rational beings. In their decision making, these politicians weigh the reality of political cost against potential political benefits. Thus political elites make choices that maximize their political and economic benefits and respectively reduce such costs.[28] Internal and external incentives that reduce the political cost of providing appropriate institutions to promote human security needs must be created. As is often the case in Africa, there appears to be a positive relationship between political power and economic power. Many political elites, who hitherto were down the economic ladder, have had their economic status dramatically improved; these elites have become millionaires and billionaires since becoming public officials. It is therefore not surprising that most people in the developing world equate wealth to politics, and would prefer to pursue a political career as a means to improve their economic well-being. People in the developing world have come to realize that having the requisite education and training alone is not a guarantee for success. Tensions, threats, and instability loom every election year as a result. Even before the electorates go to the voting booths on Election Day, the campaign period most often witnesses insecurities, and sometimes bloodshed in hotly contested electoral constituencies or districts; some people have also sustained serious life-threatening injuries due to election violence. Others are incarcerated because of their political beliefs and orientations. Kenya's elections in 2007 and

Zimbabwe's elections in 2008 are classic examples of how the electoral process, which is supposed to result in civility within the society, ends up leaving indelible physical, psychological, and emotional scars on people.

In the midst of the chaos of domestic insecurities, political elites have a responsibility to establish institutions that ensure human security since those institutions, in turn, reduces their political cost and increases their political and economic benefits. There is a positive internal and external incentive for political elites to vigorously create sustainable institutions that allow them to steer clear of domestic threats to themselves as well as the citizens they govern. Secondly, promoting human security actually sets up the stability that states need to develop and compete on the global market. The mass movement of highly skilled intellectuals and semi-skilled human resources from the developing to the developed world to seek "greener pastures" is related to the lack of human security that results from non-existent opportunities for empowerment and progress to their lives. Providing incentives to political elites to enable them to pursue policies that institutionalize human security need not come from external sources.[29] It takes political will and vision for leaders to incentivize themselves. The provision of resources for research and development, improvement of infrastructure, creating employment, expanding education, and strengthening the rule of law are investments that tend to benefit a wider percentage of the population. It also puts the nation on the path to development. Leaders who are worried about their economic survival when they leave public office will soon realize that the effective policies they have put in place to enhance human security have empowered their people, increased the trust the people have in the government, and created an effective demand within the economy. This could enable them establish their own private businesses and consulting firms after they have left office. Empowering the people and increasing the trust in government will also help alleviate the all-too-frequent allegations of abuse of power that leaders are plagued with when they leave public office.[30] When such outcomes provide enough incentives to political leaders, over the long term, those policies will be institutionalized, human security will be promoted, and development objectives attained.

On a much broader scale, the inability to establish institutional structures that promote human security has negative effect on countries in the region. Mass movement of people from one country to the other as a result of domestic human insecurities has consequences on the security of the region. For instance, the fragile situation that exists in the border region of Uganda, Kenya, Rwanda, Burundi, and the Democratic Republic of Congo is as a result of human security problems. It has created insecurities in the border regions of these states. In November of 2012, the international community accused the Rwandan president, Paul Kagame, for supporting the M23 rebel fighters to temporarily take over Goma in DR Congo. This accusation led to the United States and Canada threatening to pull financial resources that support about 40 percent of Rwanda's annual budget. When institutions that promote human security are non-existent, it could be a challenge to domestic security even in states of the developed world. Xenophobic attitudes that emerged in South Africa in 2008 and 2009 which resulted in assaults on Zimbabwean refugees further demonstrates regional implications of human security problems. This situation could strain relationship between governments in the region, as well as channel financial and other resources that are needed for developmental projects to address refugee issues and other disputes.

The developed world has a role to play regarding integrated networks that promote human security. Interdependence of the global economy necessitates that human security becomes a priority for all. Though Realists and Liberals have divergent views regarding the relationship between interdependence and global peace, Dale Copeland argued, in his theory of trade expectation, that both the liberals and the realists are right since, though economic interdependence ensures relatively stable global peace, the lack of future trade expectations could lead to war as the realists have feared.[31] However, contemporary global trends put more weight on the Liberal argument, as competition between advanced economies has led to the seeking of a favorable trade relationship with the developing world. Thus, the more improved human security that the global economy seeks in troubled states, the better it is for safer future trade relationships. Even more critical is the threat of terrorism that has emerged as a global nightmare. Developed states such as the United States, Canada, and the European Union have recognized the importance of focusing on improving the lives of people in weak and poor states so they cannot be recruited by terrorist organizations. The United States and the North Atlantic Treaty Organization's (NATO) efforts in Iraq[32] and Afghanistan, and now the US involvement in Africa, are all aimed at empowering governments to improve the dignity of their citizens.

Human security need not be viewed as a long wish list where activists hijack the concept and justify their funding sources. Many have already criticized the human security concept as being vague, ineffective, and lacking any prospect for theoretical analysis.[33] The definitions and explanations of the seven human security elements identified in the 1994 UNDP Human Development Report have spawned numerous researches on how to effectively measure its components and apply the concept within the context of contemporary security challenges that states face. The UNDP's list is, however, not exhaustive. Human needs continue to expand as new challenges arise. The definitions could also be expanded. For instance, in the 1994 Human Development Report, the economic security focuses on the availability of income from paid employment and nationally funded safety nets. The reality is that not all advanced states are effectively capable of providing such nationally funded safety nets. In the United States unemployment and homelessness present economic and social challenges. Creating appropriate institutions that promote an enabling environment where individuals establish, or team up with others to establish better lives for themselves become imperative. The availability of training programs to suit foreseeable demands would be critical, as well as confidence in laws that protect business contracts.

In examining human security in post-conflict Sierra Leone, this book focuses on four security elements, namely political, civil, economic, and personal securities.[34] These four human security elements focus on the core institutional underpinnings of stability within states of which other securities such as food, environment, and community could be achieved. In the post-conflict, because confidence and trust is at its lowest level, strategies that signal the environment is once again a level ground that ensures equal opportunities, rewards, and advancement for all people become imperative.

Human Security Situation in Sierra Leone during the War

The 1990s were a watershed in the history of Sierra Leone. Not even the post-independent era of the 1960s to the 1980s could match the intensity of fear and despair that engulfed the Sierra Leonean people. The war had a heavy toll on the people, and it affected all levels of institutions and structures. Traditional institutions such as the chieftaincy institution were disrupted. Many of the chiefs had to flee their villages and towns to seek refuge in Freetown and other big cities. People have relied on the chiefs and elders for local development projects, adjudication of justice, and security.

In 1997 disgruntled Sierra Leone army officers staged a coup to overthrow the late Ahmad Tejan Kabbah. Jonny Paul Koroma became the leader of the new ruling military Council. He invited the leader of the RUF, Forday Sankoh, to join him. This gave the rebels free access to every part of the country. As a result incidences of rape murder, maiming, and looting increased in the country.

The educational system suffered too as a result of the rebels taking over school structures and literally closing those schools. Some of the students were forced to join the rebel group as soldiers. Small arms were also proliferated as many people joined the Kamajors—a grassroots militia force—to protect the neighborhood from rebel incursions. This was a time of extreme insecurities in Sierra Leone.

Press freedom and other civil rights were curtailed by the Armed Forces Revolutionary Council (AFRC) prompting mass rejection of the military junta by civil society organizations such as women's organizations, student unions, and journalist associations.

The job situation was very bleak. Ambassador Hirsch visited the Kono region and remarked "I saw a Bruegel version of hell, with hundreds of young men moving huge piles of dirt from one open pit to another, looking in the tailings, the remnants of ground other miners had already scoured many times"[35] sums it all. Ambassador Hirsch further noted that "at the end of 1995 there was virtually no formal economic activity in the country"[36] which further collapsed the Sierra Leonean economy.

Large internal displacement of people in the country and some seeking refugee status in states such as Liberia and Guinea were reported. For the period of the war, a quarter of the Sierra Leonean population of about six million who have been displaced as IDPs and refugees lost their land, homes, and work basically affecting their financial and economic well-being.

NOTES

1. See Milton Esman. 2004. "Ethnic pluralism: Strategies for Conflict Management." In *Facing Ethnic Conflicts: Toward a New Realism*. A. Wimmer, et al. (eds.) Lanham, MD: Rowman & Littlefield Publishers, Inc.

2. See Donald Rothchild. 2004. "Liberalism, Democracy, and Conflict Management: The African Experience." In *Facing Ethnic Conflicts: Toward a New Realism*. A. Wimmer, et al. (eds.) Lanham, MD: Rowman & Littlefield Publishers, Inc., 226–44.

3. See Arend Lijphart. 1977. *Democracy in Plural Societies*. New Haven, CT: Yale University Press; Also Donald Horowitz. 2004. "Some Realism about Constitutional Engineering." In *Facing Ethnic Conflicts: Toward a New Realism*. A. Wimmer, et al. (eds.) Lanham, MD: Rowman & Littlefield Publishers, Inc., 245–57.

4. See Arend Lijphart. 1977. *Democracy in Plural Societies*. New Haven, CT: Yale University Press, pp. 49–53; 160–70

5. See I. O'Flynn and Donald Russell (ed.) 2005. *Power-Sharing: Institutional and Social Reform in Divided Societies*. London: Pluto Press.

6. The majoritarian rule has been the yardstick for electing and legitimizing political and public leadership for a state. However, translating the majority power into broad-based state objective has been problematic and challenging in the developing world. This has led to the minority been ignored and marginalized.

7. See E. A. Henderson. 2002. *Democracy and War: The End of an Illusion?* Boulder, CO: Lynne Rienner Publishers, Inc.; see also Barry R. Posen. 1993. "The Security Dilemma and Ethnic Conflict." In Michael E. Brown (ed.) *Ethnic Conflict and International Security*. Princeton, NJ: Princeton University Press.

8. The assumption could be that once implemented, the system would take care of everyone.

9. For the purpose of this study, i.e., within the context of post-conflict reconstruction, human security connotes political, civil, personal, and economic securities that secures human dignity and empowers the individual person.

10. See Mahbub ul Haq. 1994. "New Imperatives of Human Security," RGICS Paper No. 17, Rajiv Gandhi Institute for Contemporary Studies. New Delhi: Rajiv Gandhi Foundation. Dr. Mahbub-ul-Haq was a Pakistani economist and game theorist. He was also involved in developing a human development theory, and was the founder of the Human Development Report.

11. These are some form of regular cash payments the rebels receive for their services as fighters, and also in-kind perks through looting.

12. See Mahmood Mamdani. 1992. "The Peasant Question and the Contemporary Question" In Kennett, David and Tukumbi Lumumba-Kasongo (eds.) *Structural Adjustment and the*

Crisis in Africa: Economic and Political Perspective. New York: The Edwin Mellen Press. Also Anirudh Krishna, et al. (eds.) 1997. *Reasons for Hope: Instructive Experiences in Rural Development*. Herndon, VA: Kumarian Press.

13. See Wilfred I. David. 2004. *The Humanitarian Development Paradigm: Search for Global Justice*. Lanham, MD: University Press of America, Inc., p. ix.

14. See Amartya Sen. 1999. *Development as freedom*. New York: Anchor Books, pp. 38–40.

15. See James D. Fearon. 1995. "Rationalists Explanations for War." *International Organization*, Vol. 49, No. 3 (Summer 1995), pp. 379–414. Also Bruce Bueno de Mesquita. 1981. *The War Trap*. New Haven, CT: Yale University Press, p. 129.

16. See Robert D. Kaplan. 2000. *The Coming Anarchy: Shattering the Dreams of the post-Cold War*. New York: Random House Inc. Also Nicholas Sambanis. 2001. "Do Ethnic and Nonethnic Civil Wars have the same causes:? A Theoretical and Empirical Inquiry (Part 1)." *The Journal of Conflict Resolution*, Vol. 45, No. 3 (June), pp. 259–82.

17. See http://www1.voanews.com/english/news/a-13-2008-04-15-voa61-66747377.html.

18. See lecture Series on African Security titled "Nigeria's Niger Delta: Understanding the Complex drivers of Conflict." http://www.foi.se/upload/project/Africa/Obi%20Nigeria's%20 Niger%20Delta.pdf.

19. See Bruce M. Russett and John R. Oneal. 2001. *Triangulating Peace: Democracy, Interdependence, and International Organization*. New York: Norton.

20. These institutions may include the military, police, disregarding rule of law, etc.

21. See *Human Security Report 2005: War and Peace in the 21st Century*. New York: Oxford University Press. www.hsrgroup.org/human-security-reports/2005/text.aspx

22. See R. Thakur and E. Newman. 2004. (eds.) *Broadening Asia's Security and Discourse Agenda*. Tokyo: United Nations University Press.

23. See Lloyd Axworthy. 1997. "Canada and Human Security: The Need for Leadership." *International Journal*, Vol. 52, pp. 183–96.

24. States are prominent actors in achieving human security.

25. In 2001, the Commission worked to popularize the concept of humanitarian intervention which many see as an assault on state sovereignty.

26. Legitimacy of states coming out of conflict is usually reflected in the mixed feelings that citizens have in those governments. This lack of confidence leads to latent rejection of governments by the citizens. This could be corrected by committed actions on the part of governments to restore confidence in areas that promote human security.

27. See Ali Mazrui. 1999. "African Security: the Erosion of the state and the decline of Race as a basis for Human Relations." In *Globalization, Human Security and the African Experience*. Caroline Thomas and Peter Wilkin (eds.) Boulder, CO: Lynne Rienner publishers, Inc., p. 163.

28. See Anthony Downs. 1957. *An Economic Theory of Democracy*. New York: Harper.

29. This could be government or NGO sources.

30. The potential for such investigations could make elites to want to unnecessarily hold on to public office.

31. See Dale C. Copeland. 1999. "Economic Interdependence and War: A Theory of Trade Expectation," *International Studies*, Vol. 20 No. 4 (Spring), 5–41.

32. United States intervention in Iraq in 2003 is seen as an assault on a sovereign state; though insecurities still persist in the country, US investments have helped establish the rule of law and created an enabling environment for Iraqis to improve their lives. This assertion is still debateable.

33. See Florini and Simmons. 1998. "The New Security Thinking: A Review of the North American Literature," pp. 29–33. Here the authors discuss the realist view and objections to human security

34. See Agostinho Zacarias. 2003. "Redefining Security." In *From Cape to Congo: Southern Africa's Evolving Security Challenges*. Mwesiga Baregu and Christopher Landsberg (eds.) Boulder, CO: Lynne Rienner Publishers, Inc., 31–52. Zacarias identified the 4 pillars of human security as order, justice, peace, and economics.

35. See John L. Hirsch. 2001. *Sierra Leone: Diamonds and the Struggle for Democracy.* Boulder, CO: Lynne Reinner Publishers, Inc., p. 25

36. Ibid.

Chapter Three

Political and Civil Reforms

Conflicts are not perennial phenomena. They occur when the political and the governing processes become dysfunctional.[1] This chapter has three objectives: it discusses the politics of post-independent Sierra Leone up to the start of the civil war in 1991. Secondly, it establishes the reality of the political and societal relations that the post-conflict political reforms need to address. It further discusses the post-conflict political reforms including issues of rule of law. Finally, it discusses reforms in civil rights and liberties that affect human security in post-conflict Sierra Leone.

POLITICAL AND CIVIL REFORMS

The democratic political process creates an organizing structure for societies, and has been a mechanism to ensure stability and progress.[2] In contemporary societies, this process sets the framework by which citizens of states follow established rules for civility with regard to the relationship between the leadership and the governed, and the management and distribution of resources. While states in advanced democracies have mastered the process and continue to enjoy its benefits, states in Africa that have adopted the democratic process have rather seen the process divide and destroy lives, marginalize certain sections of society, and ruin infrastructure and resources of states. This situation raises an important question as to whether or not political elites and the electorate perceive the (democratic) process as legitimate means for instituting order, fairness, and progress in the society.[3]

Election campaigns are marked by high security concerns. However, this cannot be compared to the immediate after-election periods when tensions are extremely high and when political parties that lost the elections reject the election results and urge their supporters to protest such results. The aftermath of the 2007 and 2008 elections and Kenya and Zimbabwe, respectively, are classical examples of the magnitude of such post-election violence. Good stewardship and accountability on the part of political elites to serve their people have been replaced by corruption, favoritism, nepotism, threats, and insecurities within states.

The political history of most African states is characterized by structural inconsistencies, reflected in the dysfunction of the social and political process.[4] This was one of the major causes of the conflict in Sierra Leone. People's expectations, including political expectations, shape their behavioral patterns and reactions. Such expectations and reactions create the framework for action on the part of political leaders who respond by establishing effective institutions for progress. Political leaders (elected democratically or not) have or should have incentives to create such institutions that ensure consistencies in the behavior of the state as inconsistencies jeopardize internal political stability as well as the security of the entire region.[5]

Political and civil reforms, though challenging, are critical pieces of the stabilizers needed in the post-conflict. Political reforms address issues of legitimacy and the government's readiness to protect the country's territorial integrity. In Sierra Leone this becomes imperative because of the damage done to the country as a result of the spill-over of the war in neighboring Liberia. Political reforms also create the environment that the state belongs to the people, and that it is the people who make choices regarding who their leaders should be. Civil reforms reinforce political reforms, in that it helps to eradicate fears and suspicions in government activities. It creates an atmosphere of fairness through the application of the rule of law and the ability to express oneself freely without the fear of any repercussions. Obviously, if people are to choose their leadership, they do not expect those leaders to be bullies or tyrants.

SIERRA LEONE'S POLITICAL LANDSCAPE

Sierra Leone's pre-conflict political environment raises concerns and other triggers which, by all standards, signaled the dangers ahead for the state. Blatant willingness on the part of political leaders to violently oppress some ethnicities while empowering others was one of the leading structural dysfunctions of the Sierra Leonean state.[6] While independence was a collective effort, the few political elites hijacked state apparatus and resources after independence was achieved. Scholars have noted that such elite behaviors are legacies of the colonial administration that were bequeathed to the ruling class after independence.[7] Political development in Sierra Leone since independence in 1961 was consistently characterized by sporadic instability, interspersed with both civilian and military rule; the country has also witnessed both elected and unelected power-hungry and ruthless leaders emerge.[8] It is important to mention that there seem to be no difference between the leadership styles of both "democratically" elected leaders and those that assume power through military takeover of government in terms of the policies to improve the lives of the Sierra Leone people. This non-distinction between the two is disturbing since it erodes not only the confidence in the ideals of democracy experienced in other states, but also glooms the future of any political dialogue or process—a serious human security concern. The leadership styles of both civilian and military leaders are an indication of an institutional crisis that had been ignored over the years. Such an institutional crisis provided benefits to the elites who maintained the status quo.

Sierra Leone: 1961–2002

As with many other independent African states on the day of independence, Sierra Leone rose at the dawn of April 27, 1961, to realize that their hard-fought battle for independence had yielded positive results and subsequently the Sierra Leonean people and their leaders were in control of the political, economic, social, and cultural destinies of the country. However, missed opportunities on the part of the political leadership of the country resulted in ineffective policies to the amazement and disappointment of the Sierra Leonean people. Though the Sierra Leonean state is characterized as a penetrated state due to pressure from external influences such as Britain, International Organizations, non-governmental organizations (NGOs), mercenaries,[9] overwhelming evidence point to internal structural dysfunction that incapacitate the leadership and force them to put aside the security of the Sierra Leonean people and concentrate on their personal parochial security and interests.

When Albert Margai succeeded his brother, Milton Margai, in 1964 the euphoria of independence had faded away and the strong ethno-regional tendency has begun to shape the narrative of who should be in control of the political power and how much groups would be willing to compromise and coexist. To hold on to his position as the head of state, Albert Margai centralized and consolidated power by establishing an authoritarian rule. It was clear that negotiating between power consolidation and societal stability was a dilemma. This challenge is still prevalent not only in Sierra Leone but many other African states. Many of these states are burdened with which institutional options could achieve these twin objectives. This also exposes the concept and nature of security in Sierra Leone. Does security have to do with securing the elite, or the entire state and its people? Sierra Leone's political history suggests that the elite put a greater premium on their own security than that of the people and the state in general. This is reflected in the way the elite pay less attention to developing a broad-based approach to security. Effort to create legitimate institutions that provide security to the majority of the people has not been a priority. For example, Albert Margai, in an attempt to secure his power, stuffed his government with his own ethno-regional group. This further created division and tension in Sierra Leone.

The 1960s were a watershed in African politics and government. The military, through coup d'états, assumed the helm of governing several African states. It recorded six military takeovers of government involving states like Ghana, Nigeria, Central African Republic, Upper Volta (now Burkina Faso), and Burundi. The overthrow of the Ghanaian president, Kwame Nkrumah,[10] in 1996 was a defining moment of Albert Margai's presidency as he came to realize the vulnerability of his position as head of state vis-à-vis the ability of his own military to overthrow him. Margai was forced to be on the defensive as the military challenged the legitimacy of other regimes in Africa.[11] Realizing this threat to his regime, Albert Margai purged the Sierra Leonean army and made the Mende people (his own ethnicity) dominate the leadership as well as the rank-and-file of the army. However, and contrary to Albert Margai's expectation, the Mende ethnic group was fragmented. Disunity existed between Margai's Mende group from the Moyamba district and the Mendes from the Kenema district. Thus, though Margai purged the army, his actions did not result in a better pay-off since his own Mende army corps overthrew him during the 1967 elections.[12]

Siaka Stevens and his All People's Congress (APC) won the 1967 elections but had to wait for a year before his government could assume office due to a military coup by David Lansana, the Force commander, and later the National Reformation Council (NRC) who deposed Lansana in another military coup two days later. In April 1968, Siaka Stevens was finally restored to power in another military coup d'état. At this point the balance of power had tipped in favor of the northerners who dominated both the political front and the military when the entire military corps and the police leadership (mostly dominated by the Mende) were arrested and imprisoned. When Stevens assumed power, he had learned so much from the misfortunes of his predecessor that he was not ready to be controlled by the military. Challenged by the dominant northern ethnic group, the Temne, he quickly purged the military of the Temne and created an officer corps dominated by the many small and less powerful ethnic groups including the Limba (where he is from), Krio, Koranko, Yalunka, and Susu, among others. Stevens's strong desire to ensure stability and yet hold on to power in Sierra Leone ironically led to the adoption of authoritarian tactics such as arrests, detentions, and extrajudicial executions of his critics. Siaka Stevens's power consolidation strategy was influenced by his perception that Sierra Leone's society was too fragmented to rule with a consensus and unanimity, and also the belief that constitutional rule is implausible in such an environment.[13] Such was the fear of his own security[14] that in his memoir, *What Life Has Taught Me,* he acknowledged that his seventeen-year regime was preoccupied with securing his own government to the detriment of any substantive political and profound economic strategy for development. The patronage system was deeply entrenched during Stevens's rule with bribery, corruption, nepotism, and +favoritism characterizing the dependent on the very minority of the population.[15]

When Ahmed Tejan Kabbah was elected president in 1996, he also could not resist the temptation of consolidating power by courting the Kamajors, a civil defense force. The military junta that ousted the Kabbah government alleged that the Kabbah regime favored the Kamajors and for that matter rewarded them with the deputy defense minister position. Hinga Norman[16] used that position to recruit and incorporate the Kamajors into the army thereby dislodging the regular army of the privileges they enjoyed before. The Kamajors were well funded by Kabbah's government and this alienated him from the disgruntled army. The army eventually overthrew the Kabbah regime in May 1997.

The inability of Sierra Leone's political elites to professionally execute their political responsibilities was a critical underlying cause of war in the country. This blatant and sheer disregard to issues of human security by political elites resulted in the volatility of political stability within the Sierra Leonean state between the period of 1964 and well into the period 1991–2002 when the war was officially declared ended. Leaders of post-colonial Sierra Leone have not taken issues of human security seriously. While the Sierra Leonean people were excluded from the political process, development policies were also not vigorously pursued to create an enabling environment for the people to develop themselves and to improve upon their personal advancement. The military's role was not clearly defined to focus on protecting the territorial integrity of Sierra Leone.[17] The military was basically used internally to secure the selfish power consolidation of political elites. The military establishment came to the realization that it is the only entity that could ensure stability. Thus, why could it not take over power and govern as well?

When leadership culture shows a consistent behavior irrespective of whether leaders come to power through the ballot box or military take-over, the underlying explanation suggests either an existent fundamental latent institution at work, or a non-existent or dysfunctional institutional setting. It is interesting and also very difficult to explain what happened to elites' mind-set regarding governing, human security and development, and the total disregard and marginalization of the Sierra Leonean people. Brigadier David Lansana[18] had a bitter experience when he realized that even his own people, the Mendes, could not form a cohesive unit and he was ousted when he tried to cease power to prevent Siaka Stevens from assuming office right after Siaka Stevens won the 1967 general elections.[19] Thus, and as the Sierra

Leone conflict literature reveals, the cause of the civil war in Sierra Leone could be blamed on political elites, who for the lack of vision, were preoccupied with their personal interest to hold on to power to the detriment of the security and development of their own people and the state.

POLITICAL REFORMS IN POST-CONFLICT SIERRA LEONE

Arguably, the high concentration of power was one of the major causes of the conflict in Sierra Leone. The ruthless political leadership of Siaka Stevens[20] and his amendment of the country's constitution in 1978 to make Sierra Leone a single-party state stifled openness in governance and the political process. Siaka Stevens at the end of his term in 1985 hand-picked Major-General Joseph Saidu Momoh as his successor, who literally continued his predecessor's political system of single-partyism until 1991 when he amended the constitution to return the country to a multi-party system. This reform was too late since corruption had rendered his government weak and state institutions dysfunctional.[21] With the spate of military takeovers of government, rebel invasion of the country, and some multi-party political arrangements between the period of 1991 to 2002, there is no doubt that the Sierra Leonean people are looking for answers with regard to the role of politics and government and the effect on peace, order, and development within the Sierra Leonean society.

Sierra Leone is a constitutional democracy. The 1991 Constitution which has been subsequently amended over the years is the highest governing document of the land. It describes the government type as well as the rights and responsibilities of citizens. The branches of government include the executive, legislative, and the judiciary. The president is the head of state and head of government. Cabinet appointments are made by the president and approved by the legislature based on majority vote. The legislature is unicameral with 124 members of which 112 are elected representatives of the existing political parties, and 12 are paramount chiefs elected in separate elections to serve a period of five years. The judicial branch is made up of the Supreme Court, Court of Appeals, High Courts, and Magistrate courts. Local chieftaincy courts with judges that administer cases involving customary laws are also part of the judiciary system.

Since the conflict was officially declared ended in 2002, the government of Sierra Leone has undertaken numerous political reforms with support from the United Nations Development Program (UNDP), the British government through the Department for International Development (DfID), and the Japanese government. The Local Government Act of 2004 is one such legislative document that decentralizes political power and involves the Sierra Leonean people in the governance process.

Local Government Act of 2004

The Local Government Act of 2004 has transformed the political landscape in Sierra Leone. Decentralization and the widening of political space at numerous levels is the goal. In the early 1970s, Siaka Stevens abolished the District Assembly concept. His All People's Congress (APC) government substantially altered the country's constitution to outlaw the multiparty political system (which ironically brought him to power) and established a single-party system with the APC party as the only political party. With the coming into effect of the Local Government Act of 2004, the political environment changed from a top-down system to that of a bottom-up approach resulting in a better relationship between government and the governed. Grassroots politics is encouraged, and information flowed from the top to the bottom and bottom to the top. Government policies showed reaction to citizens' concerns and some form of partnership formed between the government and the people. Government officials at higher levels, to some extent, relied on public opinion and other information obtained from the very lower levels of government to assist in the development of broad policy objectives and equitable distribution of resources.

With the passage of the Local Government Act of 2004, district and local councils effectively came to be established to get the people involved in everyday governance issues. Councilors to the district were elected along party lines to serve and were given the responsibilities to plan, organize, and direct activities. Some of these activities include the collection of revenues through taxation, and the discharge of certain services including education and healthcare. Challenges to the political reforms, however, have included the issue of skilled manpower needed to effectively support the massive decentralization project. The low literacy rate of 35 percent[22] is a major challenge to realizing the full positive impact of the political reforms. During the eleven years of the conflict, educational facilities were used as rebel camps and headquarters. Some were also destroyed by rebels; this greatly disrupted educational activities.

Local Council

The Local Government Act of 2004 widened the political space in Sierra Leone by authorizing the president, upon recommendation from the Ministry of Finance and National Electoral Commission, to establish a council for a locality.[23] According to paragraph a-d of subsection (3) of section (2) of the Local Government Act of 2004, local councils may be established based on the population size and density of the locality and the anticipated future population growth. The local council is to be a body corporate.[24] The local council also becomes the highest body charged with the responsibility of mobilizing resources within the locality, and to incorporate governmental agencies and other stakeholders that are sympathetic to the development of the locality. A local council in a locality shall consists of not less than twelve members made up of the chairperson, chiefs selected by the paramount chiefs within the specified locality,[25] and other members duly elected into the Council. The other members of the Council should be affiliated to one of the existing political parties, or run as an independent. Council members also serve a term of four years when elected. The council conducts its business, which is usually opened to the public, once every month and chaired by the Chairperson. Two important committees are critical for the operation of the Council and also to allow the Council's operations to meet the needs of the people. The first is the Development Planning Committee, and the second is the Budgeting and Finance Committee.

Among the functions of the local council, as stipulated in Article 20 (2) of the Local Government Act of 2004 include:

1. to mobilize the human and material resources necessary for the overall development and welfare of the people in the locality;
2. to promote and support productive activity and social development in the locality;
3. to initiate and maintain programmes for the development of basic infrastructure and provide works and services in the locality;
4. to be responsible for the development, improvement, and management of human settlements and the environment in the locality;
5. to initiate, draw up, and execute development plans for the locality;
6. to coordinate and harmonize the execution of programs and projects promoted or carried out by public corporations, other statutory bodies, and non-governmental organizations in the locality;
7. to cooperate with relevant agencies to ensure the security of the locality;
8. to oversee chiefdom councils in the performance of functions delegated to them by the local council;
9. to determine the rates of local tax;
10. to approve the annual budgets of Chiefdom Councils and oversee the implementation of such budgets.

Article 23 also stipulates that any government ministry that plans an activity that impacts the lives of people living within a particular locality must first consult the local council for advice and approval. This particular portion of the Act reaffirms government's commitment to ensure good governance within the Sierra Leonean society. Most surveys regarding the underlying cause(s) of the conflict in Sierra Leone have noted that one of the major causes of the conflict was that Sierra Leoneans perceived the government as detached from the realities of the issues that impact citizens' daily lives. When the root cause of conflict is traced to the lack of or decay of social structures and institutions, such structures and institutions could be identified and developed to potentially enhance individual capacity and success in life—a critical element of human security.

Corruption, Accountability, and Transparency

As in many societies, corruption is a major challenge to the foundation of established institutions. By its very nature and mechanism, widespread corruption renders institutions ineffective and consequently becomes a recipe for societal breakdown. Politically, corruption affects the ability of the ruling elites to be accountable and transparent in governing. The reason being that elites' political survival and hold to public office rest not on the people but their ability to channel the resources and influence obtained through corruption to manipulate election and other political outcomes to their advantage. Corruption is an endemic problem within the Sierra Leonean society; it is one major reason why the government has been less responsive to the needs of the Sierra Leonean people. In addition to involving the Sierra Leonean people in politics and governance, the Local Government Act of 2004 also addressed the issue of accountability and transparency. The government also made it a priority to reduce or eliminate corruption at all levels.

In one aggressive public relations effort to curb corruption, giant billboards were raised and posters were put up across the country to educate citizens that corruption is a crime. It warns Sierra Leoneans not to engage in acts of corruption, and also to report any suspicion of acts of corruption to the Anti-Corruption Commission. Section 103 of the Local Government Act of 2004 also subjects elected officials to the provisions of the Anti-Corruption Act of 2001. Elected officials are required to provide an inventory of their assets to the Anti-Corruption Commission upon being elected. The Commission will then proceed to monitor elected officials' assets throughout their tenure in office. Any elected official convicted of corruption charges would be fined a maximum of ten million Sierra Leonean Leones or imprisoned for a maximum of three years or both.[26] This is novel, though, for Sierra Leone to put in place a proactive mechanism to fight corruption as compared to other states in Africa also fighting the corruption epidemic. In Ghana for instance, incumbent government officials are very influential which makes such a proactive mechanism very difficult. However, when government changes hands after elections, alleged corrupt government officials could be brought before court to face charges.

To ensure transparency in the activities of the local council, and to enable people in the locality to have access to the council's activities, Section 107 of the Local Government Act stipulates that the local councils should make available information regarding their activities on their notice boards or other public places. Such council information includes:

1. monthly statements of financial accounts;
2. annual income and expenditure statements;
3. inventories of assets of the local councils;
4. by-laws and notices relating to tax rates and fees;
5. minutes of council meetings; and
6. development plans.

The Local Government Act of 2004 also makes it mandatory for the local councils to make available copies of reports, notices, and statements (at a fee) when called upon to do so (Article 107 (2)).

The Institution of Chieftaincy

As part of the political decentralization process, the post-conflict political reforms have revitalized the chieftaincy institution within the Sierra Leonean society. The 12 political districts in Sierra Leone have been divided into 149 chiefdoms. Chiefdoms which are headed by a paramount chief are the basic unit of administration in Sierra Leone. Chiefs are close to the people, and as custodians of the land, they occupy a respectful and influential role within Sierra Leonean societies. The history of the institution of chieftaincy in Sierra Leone dates back to British colonial administration. As one of the strategies of indirect rule, the British colonial administration established these "chieftaincy families" and to appoint paramount chiefs to rule the hinterlands where the colonial administration could not administer effectively. Paramount chiefs were empowered to make political, social, economic, and other administrative decisions within their area of control. Though the institution of chieftaincy is widely respected in Sierra Leone and other countries such as Ghana, the British colonial administration in Sierra Leone exploited the institution which resulted in the corruption of the institution.[27] However, the chieftaincy institution is highly regarded in Sierra Leonean societies. Thus, irrespective of the challenges of the institution, most Sierra Leoneans believe that the chieftaincy system still has a role to play in any meaningful post-conflict political reforms.

Consequently, the Local Government Act, 2004, stipulates specific role for the chiefs in the post-conflict political decentralization reforms. This includes chiefs and the chieftaincy institution assisting in:

1. preventing violence within the chiefdoms;
2. prohibiting or restricting illegal gambling;
3. making and enforcing by-laws; and

4. holding land in trust for the people in the various chiefdoms

The chiefs' roles, thus, supplement that of the local council. All paramount chiefs within the locality are automatic members of the local council. In the past, chiefs were also responsible for levying taxes but that responsibility has been turned over to the local council. The paramount chief's position is achieved through elections of individuals believed to have been from a royal lineage. Paramount chiefs have also been assigned legislative roles in the Sierra Leonean Parliament. Currently, 12 seats out of the 124-member seats in the Sierra Leonean Parliament have been allocated specifically to paramount chiefs.

Village Head Man System

Also, at the very basic level of the post-conflict political reforms in Sierra Leone is the village head man system.[28] The local council appoints head men (or women) for the villages to lead the village community in educating the people regarding government projects and other civic responsibilities. Among the responsibilities of the village head men are the making of by-laws in the various villages and to enforce those laws. These by-laws are drafted with inputs from the people in the community; this process makes the implementation of these by-laws, in most cases, easier. Because the people are involved in making these laws, fewer violations of the law occur within the communities. Violation of any of the by-laws carries a heavy punitive fine. Heinous criminal acts within the community are outside the capabilities of the village head man system; such crimes are referred to the security services such as the police. The office of the village head man is non-partisan; and their responsibilities include the mobilizing of the community for political sensitization workshops, and also organizing the community to meet politicians, when given prior notice.[29] The village, which was hitherto largely ignored in the politics and governance process, has emerged as the nucleus of political engagement. The community gets the opportunity to question political leaders (example, member of Parliament and councilors) on issues that matter to them, such as why development is lagging in the village.

Village head men are also involved in the collection of tax revenues. Because these head men are well known in the community, it becomes very difficult for people to evade paying their taxes when they are approached by one of the head men. On the other hand, it is incumbent on these head men to maintain an extremely high standard of integrity to gain the respect and confidence of the community they serve. The role is clearly cut out for the incumbent; good stewardship is rewarded with praises. On the other hand, irresponsible and corrupt behaviors on the part of a head man are criticized by the same people that the head man encounters every day. The key element that anchors the head man's role is the close personal relationship he or she develops with members of the community. This relationship that is developed contrasts the head man system with the district, local, and the chieftaincy system. Though this position is a non-paid one, it is usually an incentive as it offers the head men the opportunity to test the political waters and to launch future political ambitions

Village head men were also instrumental in reintegrating ex-combatants into the community. The Demobilization, Disarmament and Reintegration (DDR) program which the government of Sierra Leone negotiated with all the parties in the eleven-year civil conflict was one of the key provisions enshrined in the Lome Peace Accord (LPA) signed in July of 1999. Some ex-combatants even carried out brutal killings and other violent acts within the community they once lived. Community members can therefore identify them. The challenge of integrating and accommodating these ex-combatants into these communities without them suffering retributions from the family members who want to avenge the death and physical harm to their relatives was daunting and also of great concern to the Sierra Leonean government. The head men system, when created, facilitated the reintegration process by enabling ex-combatants settle comfortably into the various societies. The head man vouches for new behaviors of the ex-combatants, making it easier for ex-combatants to live within the community.

Reforms, Institutions, and Challenges

Sierra Leone's political reforms signify the commitment by Sierra Leone's political elites to address the issue of political marginalization and the remoteness of government from the people. This was one of the major causes of the conflict. The reform has the goal of bringing politics to the doorsteps of the people and to encourage participation. However, such reforms face tough challenges and could even be derailed when measures to strengthen accountability are not put in place. This could further marginalize women, the youth, and the poor who are the very people such reforms were meant to benefit.[30] Harold Lasswell famously defined politics as who gets what, when, and how. The political system and process, no doubt, is the conduit for resource distribution and becomes even more pronounced in developing countries where most resources are under government control. In a fragile political environment, like that of Sierra Leone, the challenge becomes how these new institutions could withstand the realities of the times. Among these realities are the high expectations that the political reforms should instantly result in a positive impact on the economic conditions of the average Sierra Leonean. Accountability and transparency become critical for positive action. The system of how aid in any form at the local level could be effective, it is argued that without accountability and transparency similar to that required of the legislature, basic development goals and implementation becomes a private good that is controlled by only a few people.[31] There is always the tendency that few people who have gained access to the local resources will exploit them for their personal gains and subsequently institutionalize the patronage system that favors some group and marginalize others, now and in the future.

The Local Government Act of 2004 made significant role changes with regard to the power and influence of traditional authorities. Chiefs had tremendous powers during pre-independence Sierra Leone. They controlled the land resources as well as the power to levy taxes to develop their various communities. These powers were reduced immediately after independence in 1961 until Siaka Stevens abolished the local government system in 1972 and restored chiefs' powers, including that of land control and taxes. The search for an appropriate role for the chiefs in the reform process was a daunting task. Several forums including consultations and workshops led by the Department for International Development (DfID) were organized to define the role of the chieftaincy system in Sierra Leone. Unfortunately, many Sierra Leoneans were not satisfied with the past role of the chiefs and brought negative allegations against the chieftaincy system, which include the mismanagement of resources, corruption in the delivery of local justice, and the discrimination against women and other underprivileged individuals such as the youth. Thus, the Local Government Act of 2004 gave the revenue-collection role of the chiefs to the local council. However, chiefs continued to make and enforce by-laws within their communities and continue to hold land in trust for the people in the chiefdoms.

The idea that a chief be elected to that position creates a challenge regarding where the loyalty of the chief really lies, and whose interest the chief would eventually serve. In the first place, the concept of chieftaincy in Sierra Leone is no different from the concept held in some other African states such as Ghana that has established chieftaincy institutions. Chiefs basically are custodians of the land, and are in fact the representatives of the ancestors and spirits that rule and own the land. The chief's ruling power is, thus, derived from traditional legitimacy. Contemporary election processes generally create faction groups vying for position of control. This comes with the control of decision making and the management of limited resources. In this regard, the election process itself threatens the traditional legitimacy of the chieftaincy institution as is currently the case in Sierra Leone. This could explain why DfID's consultation in 2003 to discuss a substantive role for the chiefs within decentralized Sierra Leone was overwhelmed with negative comments regarding the system itself. Chiefs know who they are accountable to. As rational actors, leadership survival is the goal and that influences their decision-making. Thus coalitions and/or institutions that support that goal are more likely to secure a chief's allegiance. Unfortunately, ordinary people may be left out in the discussion. An institutional crisis could result even at the basic level of governance following this confusion. The challenge then becomes how to fuse traditional belief systems with the realities of contemporary political struggles.

BOTTOM LINE: IMPACT OF THE POLITICAL REFORMS?

The immediate post-conflict era is embedded with high expectations, especially in cases where the previous government was a dictatorship and suppressed citizens' rights to participate in the political process. This could be seen not just in Africa but other parts of the world. In Africa, the new enabling political environment in the immediate after-conflict is marked by high voter participation in countries such as Egypt, Zimbabwe, South Africa, South Sudan, Ghana, and Sierra Leone. However, the mere participation in the voting process is not enough to sustain a positive feeling of the process. How people feel about their participation is critical to sustain the process. The feeling barometer could range from how participating in the political process impacts people's lives to how it enhances the welfare of the community. Sierra Leoneans still question whether they are really part of the democratic process, and whether the decentralization program is something worth having confidence in, in spite of increased participation. The decentralization process has been very slow than anticipated. A number of organizations, including international NGOs such as Action Aid, have lamented about the extremely slow pace of the decentralization process. A survey by Action Aid found that five years after the implementation of the decentralization program, most Sierra Leoneans are not participants of local government's activities, thereby making them lose confidence in the operations of the local government.[32] Thus, the objective of the devolution of power has not yet been realized. The administration in Freetown is still in control of the organization, decision making and finances of the local council.[33] Communication, on the other hand, has improved greatly between the local council and the central administration. The main concern is communication between the Local Council and the community they serve.

Officials charged with the responsibility of overseeing and implementing the decentralization program have consistently argued that the process need more time to take effect and for it to work effectively. They also acknowledge that people's attitude and the lack of much needed resources and capacity have negatively slowed down the process. In the post-conflict era, where people's participation in government has been identified as a priority, adequate resources are needed to ensure participation and transparency in the political process. In June 2009, a local newspaper in Freetown quoted the vice president of the Republic of Sierra Leone, Alhaji Samuel Sam-Sumana, expressing his dismay at what he calls "the slow pace at which the decentralization process is going."[34] This was at a workshop to re-launch the devolution process entirely again and to bring to speed the activities of entities that are supposed to spearhead the process. In 2009, five years after the Local Council Act of 2004 was promulgated and put into operation, local councils are still lagging in its service delivery responsibilities. The performance of the local councils has not been reviewed yet to determine whether objectives are being met, and whether there is the need for a change in strategy. The vice president's call is a wake-up one for all stakeholders involved in the decentralization process. In attendance at the workshop were the Sierra Leone's Decentralization Secretariat (Dec-Sec), United Nations Development Programme (UNDP), and the United Nations Capital Development Fund (UNCDF).

The question therefore is why, in spite of the fact that relevant stakeholders have been involved, the much-needed devolution of the political process that enables the Sierra Leonean people to be actively involved and also to ensure the implementation of good governance has not been achieved. Stakeholders such as the UNDP, DfID, ECOWAS, and the African Union (AU) have consistently argued that good governance is critical to achieving post-conflict reconstruction sustainability and to ensure an enabling environment for growth. These same stakeholders have touted the 2002, 2007, and 2012 presidential and parliamentary elections, and the 2004 and 2008 local government elections, as successful. However, there seem to be a disconnect between what the policy documents seek to achieve, how such policies are to be implemented, and people's perception regarding the effect of the decentralization program. Many continue to question whether organizing elections is what decentralization and reform is all about. They do not see any difference between the current political process and the one that existed before the war. Politicians are still detached from the ordinary citizens, and still could not understand or resonate with the current reality that the Sierra Leonean people want to be actively involved in the political process.

Civil Rights and Civil Liberties Reforms

Social injustices with the consequent violation of civil rights and liberties of the Sierra Leonean people were among the reasons for the onset of the civil war in Sierra Leone.[35] The courts either ceased to function as they could not convene to adjudicate justice, or were rendered ineffective as they became part of the executive branch, carrying on the agendas of political elites. Effective justice system was therefore imperative in post-conflict Sierra Leone to ensure true and fair justice for the Sierra Leonean people. The need to create an environment where people will have confidence in the judicial system became a priority. The Abidjan Peace Accord[36] was one of the relevant peace documents that served as a reference point. Though the Abidjan Peace Accord hit a road block as a result of the coup in Sierra Leone in 1996 and the subsequent overthrow of the Kabbah's government in May 1997 by the Armed Forces Revolutionary Council (AFRC),[37] its provisions, however, served as a guide to the subsequent Lome Peace Accord in 1999. Articles 19 and 20 of the Abidjan Peace Accord stipulate the need to uphold civil rights and liberties, and also to make the respect for human rights a priority.

The Abidjan Peace Accord thus placed the Sierra Leone legal system within the broader context of the Universal Declaration of Human Rights (UDHR) and the African Charter on Human and People's Rights. Some of these rights include the right to life and liberty, freedom from torture, right to a fair trial, freedom of expression and association, the freedom of conscience, and even the rights to take part in the governance of Sierra Leone, among others. The Revolutionary United Front (RUF) was also given the right to full access to the media, and the right to mobilize and demonstrate freely in Sierra Leone. The Abidjan Peace Accord was fully represented on both sides of the conflict including the presence of the late Alhaji Dr. Ahmed Tejan Kabbah, then president of Sierra Leone, and Corporal Foday Sankoh, the leader of the RUF. Also in attendance were other important stakeholders such as the UN Secretary General's special envoy to Sierra Leone, Berhanu Dinka, a representative from the OAU now AU, Ms. Adwoa Coleman, a representative from the commonwealth organization, Dr. Moses Anafu, and then president of Cote D'Ivoire, Henri Konan Bedie. The Lome Peace Accord that followed three years later, in 1999, was to reaffirm the 1996 Abidjan Peace Accord and also work out some details regarding how to practically implement the provisions outlined to end the conflict.

Sierra Leone's Human Rights Commission

In line with the African Charter of Human Rights, the Human Rights Commission of Sierra Leone (HRCSL) was established by an Act of Parliament (Act No. 9 of 2004) to protect and promote human rights among the Sierra Leonean people.[38] The idea of this Commission was highlighted in the 1999 Lome Peace Accord and was also recommended in the Truth and Reconciliation Commission (TRC) report in 2004. The Human Rights Commission was officially inducted to start operation in 2006 and became operational in 2007. The Commission's role includes ensuring a well-coordinated monitoring and enhancement of a human rights culture within the Sierra Leonean society, to advise and keep government informed about the human rights situation in the country, and also to investigate human rights violations.[39] Since it became operational, it has undertaken several activities that strengthen and protect human rights. It was noted that educating both the public and government officials as well as applying other sensitization measures (workshops, etc.)

are critical to ensure an effective achievement of the Commission's goals. The Commission is also charged with the responsibility of implementing the recommendations of the TRC.[40]

Justice Sector Reforms

Responses from individuals regarding the war show grave concerns about the justice system. Before the war started, the justice system was weak and was unable to discharge its responsibilities of addressing people's civil rights and liberties. Delays in investigations, trials, backlogs of cases, and the inability of the justice system to effectively respond to organized crimes were part of the underlying causes of the civil war. In addition to that, police and court buildings were also taken over and destroyed during the war, making it difficult for such security and justice institutions and their structures to operate effectively after the war. Reforming the justice sector is obviously a priority in post-conflict Sierra Leone.[41]

The fundamental goals of the justice sector reform are not only to ensure accessibility to the justice system, but also to restore confidence in the justice system. After years and series of deliberations and surveys, recommendations were made in 2004 for a Justice Sector Reform in Sierra Leone. The reform is in two parts: to restore the rule of law and guarantee affordable and equitable access to justice for all Sierra Leoneans; and secondly, to ensure security for Sierra Leoneans within their communities. The overall objective of the Justice Sector Reform is to provide opportunities that ensure that personal and business grievances are addressed properly in order to create an enabling environment for safety and security, economic growth, and reduction in poverty. These objectives are imperative to enhance human security and promote human dignity. Results of a Security Sector Review (SSR) conducted by the Office of National Security (ONS) in 2004 indicated that the Sierra Leonean people have lost confidence in the justice system. The government consequently noted the situation as one of the potential threats to the post-conflict recovery. The Sierra Leonean government is committed to these reforms because it sees it as integral to conflict prevention and poverty reduction. After a comprehensive study, the government of Sierra Leone in 2007 outlined a three year (2008–2010) Justice Sector Reform Strategy and Investment Plan.[42]

The vision of the reform document was "A Sierra Leone where there is safety for people, security of property and access to justice." The reform was to better coordinate the relationship between existing stakeholders such as the police service, prisons service, and the judiciary which has, in the past, either operated differently or was rendered ineffective by political interferences. The vision of the Justice Sector Reform and Investment Plan acknowledges the critical role of government to ensure accessibility and fair means of dealing with crime, conflicts, disputes, and grievances. The vision has three main focuses. Firstly, it was realized that the formal system of justice was not accessible to about 70 percent of the people.[43] Hence, the priority was to refocus the delivery of justice into the community at the chiefdom levels. Secondly, it was realized that there was an overwhelming backlog of cases that needed to be adjudicated. Based on this evidence, the strategy was to enhance coordination, cooperation, and communication between all sectors involved in the justice system delivery. Thirdly, the vision also welcomes civil society organizations to serve as watchdogs to independently ensure the effective operation of the reformed justice system. The Sierra Leonean government would thus consider any contribution from civil society organizations regarding how to make the justice system better in the post-conflict era. There was no doubt the Sierra Leonean government is determined, through this reform, to co-opt its six million people to be part of the effort to revamp the justice system. By creating the avenue for civil society organizations to act as watchdogs, it encourages both the accessibility to the justice delivery system as well as the confidence in the system.

Justice Delivery System

Sierra Leone's justice system currently involves both old and new stakeholders. The old stakeholders include institutions such as the Ministry of Justice, Ministry of Internal Affairs, Ministry of Social Welfare, the police, and the prison service. Others such as the Local Government and Community Development were suspended in 1972, and the judiciary was rendered ineffective during the Siaka Stevens regime leading up to the civil war. The Gender and Children's Affairs, the Law Reform Commission, the Judicial and Legal Services Commission, and the Office of the Ombudsman are recent reform institutions to revamp the justice system and make justice accessible to different categories of Sierra Leonean society.

In addition to the roles of local agencies in the justice sector reform as outlined above, the roles of two key international organizations are also vital. The United Nations Development Programme (UNDP) and the British government's Department for International Development (DfID) have played, and continue to play, vital roles in the justice delivery system in Sierra Leone. The UNDP, through the Peace Building Fund (PBF), has supported the Sierra Leonean government to reform and revive the justice sector. The UNDP's Access to Justice Initiative supports processes and activities that enhance the speed, cost effectiveness, and efficiency in the justice delivery system. Series of workshops are organized regularly to achieve the objective of making available access to fair justice particularly to women and juveniles, and to reduce backlogs of cases in order to forestall human rights abuses. DfID has also contributed funds to help in this direction.

The Local Court System

The Local Court Act of 1963 established the local court system with jurisdiction on civil matters such as marriage and divorce, succession, land tenure, and debt payment. Sierra Leone's customary laws are the basis for adjudicating such cases, and the Constitution affirms decisions made as a result of applying customary laws. These local courts are presided over by a court chairman appointed by the paramount chief for three years and approved by the Ministry of Local Government. The decisions made at the local courts are also subject to review by the Ministry of Justice's customary law office.

In spite of the availability of the local courts as a means of settling disputes in Sierra Leonean societies, a National Public Services Delivery Survey[44] revealed that Sierra Leoneans expressed less confidence in the local court system. The UNDP[45] has also expressed concern about the same issue. The negative reviews about the court system are expressed across provinces and among the genders. Due to the lack of confidence in the local courts system, the survey noted that as high as 40 percent of cases adjudicated at the local courts are appealed. Many also cite the imposition of excessive fines and gender discriminations as areas where the courts are lagging.

The Sierra Leonean government has made the effectiveness of the court system a priority. However, the unavailability of judges vis-à-vis the increased volume of cases that are brought before the courts presents a challenge which invariably affects the final judgments.

The Chief's Court

Sierra Leone is divided into 149 chiefdoms. At the traditional level, chiefs appointed by the paramount chief are the recognizable faces of government in their localities. As the custodians of the land, chiefs have effectively created an assembly ("courts") for settling disputes, with the members of the traditional council of elders in attendance. Under the 1963 Local Government Act, affirmed by the Local Government Act of 2004, chiefs are to have jurisdiction on land and boundary disputes and not customary law issues. However, due to the suspension in 1972 of the 1963 Local Government Act and the lack of local courts at the community levels, the chiefs have filled the gap to adjudicate cases involving customary law. The chief's "court" system starts when a plaintiff approaches the chief and pays a token fee and presents his/her case. The chief then sends a summons to the defendant to appear at a location and time for judgment on an allegation. Whoever is found guilty is handed exorbitant fines to settle.

The chief's rulings on customary law issues have literally been based on local traditional practices that favor men and discriminate against women. For instance, in divorce cases, women were ejected from the family homes;

they have also been accused of practicing witchcraft. It is also alleged that men accused of rape and violence against women have been released without severe punitive sentences. These are very serious human security issues, especially where these women have suffered such discriminations before and, during the eleven-year conflict.

Criminal Justice System

The magistrate and high courts have also been reformed to deal with more serious criminal cases. Such courts systems in post-conflict Sierra Leone are critical to ensure that violent and criminal acts committed against the government and the people are prosecuted and not allowed to perpetuate. These courts are imperative and measure the extent to which the Sierra Leonean society adjudicates[46] criminal acts; this has consequence for peace and stability as well as the confidence in governmental institutions responsible for a safe society. It is also a measure of the extent to which government can provide peace and stability in the society in order to enhance the confidence that people have in the government. When Sierra Leoneans are hopeful that the rule of law actually works, and that effective justice system exist to ensure fairness and equity, human security shall be improved and development goals achieved.

Magistrate Courts

The magistrate court begins the formal criminal justice system which is responsible for prosecuting and punishing individuals that have been accused of criminal acts. The magistrate court handles most of the criminal cases that are brought to it by the Sierra Leone police. The process starts when there is an arrest of a suspect by the police, and all the necessary evidence to charge the suspect is put together. The police prosecutor brings the suspect to the magistrate court for the first hearing in front of a judge.[47] Cases are usually adjourned for hearing to a later date. The most serious criminal cases do not go through the magistrate court for first hearings; they go straight to the high court, which is the next highest level in the court system.

The problem with the magistrate courts is the persistent adjournment of cases leading to backlogs that have characterized the Sierra Leonean justice system. The adjournments are usually due to the non-availability of witnesses, unwillingness of defense counsel to follow through with the case, the failure of the accused to appear, and the lack of logistics (such as the unavailability of vehicle and personnel). This makes it difficult for the prison department to bring the accused to court. These problems negatively affect the criminal justice system. In the first place, victims are put in suspense not knowing when justice would be served. Secondly, the suspects are thrown in jail and therefore justice is denied them for a long time. This becomes even more precarious when suspects are actually innocent and have to endure deplorable jail conditions such as overcrowding, unhygienic environments, sicknesses, and emotional torments. This has serious human security implications and other negative consequences that impede the development of the people as also the overall development of the Sierra Leonean state.

High Courts

The high court is the next highest level in the court system after the magistrate court. Though the magistrate court holds most of the first hearings in criminal cases, the majority of these cases are forwarded to the high court for final adjudication.[48] Appeals are, however, forwarded to the appeals courts for consideration. Although the objective of the justice sector reform was to enable speedier access to justice, the current court establishment has not been able to keep up with the number of cases received and backlogs are still prevalent.

The magistrate and high court systems, though available, are distant from the very people that need the services. About an estimated 70 percent of the Sierra Leonean people rely on the local chiefs and elders to resolve disputed cases.[49]

Independent Organizations

Several non-governmental organizations are also involved in the civil rights and liberties reforms, mainly through the promotion of human rights in Sierra Leone. For instance, the Network Movement for Democracy and Human Rights (NMDHR) is involved in complementing the government's effort to promote human rights and good governance. Among the modus operandi of NMDHR is to report any human rights abuses to the Human Rights Commission. Also, by acting as a liaison between the government and the people, NMDHR is able to disseminate current and continuing government reforms in civil rights and liberties to remote areas in Sierra Leone, where the government's effort cannot reach. NMDHR also interprets new reform provisions where language technicalities prevent the people from fully comprehending the new civil rights available to them. The Sierra Leonean government also seeks the advice of these independent organizations to improve civil rights and liberties. In 2007, for instance, inputs from these organizations led to the development of political party code of conduct that resulted in the safe elections that year.

Quite unlike the NMDHR which provide information to the people with regard to the government's civil rights reforms, the Center for Democracy and Human Rights (CDHR), an NGO located in Makeni, the capital of the

Northern Province, acts like an advocacy organization. It promotes human rights, culture, and participatory governance at the grassroots levels through dissemination, advocacy, lobbying, dialogue forum, and civic education. It has also been actively involved in post-conflict reconstruction integrity monitoring of government supported projects that are implemented by the Sabuba and the National Commission for Social Action (NaCSA). It also monitors court proceedings and notifies judges where it believes cases are not fairly adjudicated. In addition, CDHR promotes the principle of equality before the law and provides legal services to rural women to ensure their access to fair justice.

One other important organization that promotes civil rights and liberties is the Sierra Leone Court Monitoring Programme (SLCMP), an organization established to closely monitor the proceedings at courts in Sierra Leone, the Special Court for Sierra Leone, and the implementation of the recommendations of the Truth and Reconciliation Commission. Through its activities, SLCMP has been able to convince the domestic courts to revisit cases where it believes innocent victims have been wrongly thrown into jail. One extraordinary effort by SLCMP to strengthen the reform in the area of civil rights and civil liberties is the publication of a booklet, "After you have been arrested; what next."[50] This booklet contains vital information regarding the rights of the Sierra Leonean people once someone is arrested. Some of this information includes: what is bail, the levels in the court system, the consequences of the charges against an individual, what to expect in court, and what happens at the trial, among others. This document not only educates the people as to what their rights are in the criminal justice system, it also elaborates on the excruciating trial process and what an individual is involved in when they commit a crime. When viewed critically, this booklet serves as a disincentive to criminal acts and behaviors since people are exposed to the nitty-gritty of the law and the effect on their lives.

NOTES

1. See William Reno. 1998. *Warlord Politics and the African State.* Boulder, CO: Lynne Rienner Publishers, Inc.
2. See Hobbes and Locke's perspective on social contract theory.
3. See "Legitimacy and Rule: Africa in search of a political order." Paper presented by Francis Wiafe-Amoako at the Alabama Political Science Association Conference, Samford University, Birmingham, Alabama. April 2011.
4. See William Reno. 1998. *Warlord Politics and the African State.* Boulder, CO: Lynne Rienner Publishers, Inc., p. 274
5. Ibid.
6. See Abdul Karim Bangura. 2007. "Politicized Ethnicities versus Tribal Ethnicities: Examples from Liberia, Rwanda, and Sierra Leone." In Santosh C. Saha (ed.) *The Politics of Ethnicity and National Identity.* New York: Peter Lang Publishing Inc., pp. 121–38.

7. See Claude Ake (ed.) 1985. "The state in Contemporary Africa." In *Political Economy of Nigeria*. London: Longman. p. 2; Also George Klay Kieh Jr. (ed.) 2007. *Beyond State failure and Collapse: Making the State Relevant in Africa.* Lanham, MD: Lexington Books.
8. See Juergen Dedring. 2008. *The United Nations Security Council in the 1990s: Resurgence and renewal.* Albany: State University of New York Press.
9. See Hashim Gibrill. 2007. "The Disintegration and Restoration of State Authority in Sierra Leone" In *Beyond State failure and Collapse: Making the State Relevant in Africa.* George Klay Kieh Jr. (ed.) Lanham, MD: Lexington Books.
10. Albert Margai had admired and deem Kwame Nkrumah, the first sub-Saharan African president, as an inspirer.
11. See Earl Conteh-Morgan and Mac Dixon-Fyle. 1999. *Sierra Leone at the End of the Twentieth Century: History, Politics, and Society*. New York: Peter Lang Publishing, Inc.
12. Ibid.
13. Ibid.
14. A dilemma many African leaders face' and also a paradox as to why the same mistake is repeated over and again by African political elites.
15. See the Selectorate theory in Bruce Bueno de Mesquita, et al. 2003. *The Logic of Political Survival*. Cambridge: The Massachusetts Institute of Technology Press.
16. Hinga Norman was the leader of the Kamajors, a civil defense force (CDF), who fought alongside the government army against the Revolutionary United Front (RUF) during the civil war.
17. See Conteh-Morgan and Dixon-Fyle (1999), pp. 76–89, on how the Sierra Leonean military as well as other public service agencies have been purged by successive governments to reflect their own ethnicity.
18. Brigadier David Lansana was the Force Commander during Albert Margai's regime and into the 1967 elections that saw Siaka Stevens wins the general elections. He staged a coup in March 21, 1967 on the day Siaka Stevens was sworn in and he was overthrown two days later by his own ethnic Mende military personnel.
19. See Earl Conteh-Morgan and Mac Dixon-Fyle. 1999. *Sierra Leone at the End of the Twentieth Century: History, Politics, and Society*. New York: Peter Lang Publishing, Inc., p. 80.
20. Even to the extent of sometimes murdering very close associates who helped him in diverse ways.
21. See William Reno. 1995. *Corruption and State Politics in Sierra Leone*. New York: Cambridge University Press.
22. See the CIA World Factbook http://www.cia.gov.
23. This is the administrative area of a local council which includes a district, town, city, or metropolis.
24. The council effectively assumes a legal personality that can sue and be sued.
25. Only for those localities that have a system of paramount chieftaincy. This is to represent the interest of the paramount chiefs who are assumed to be custodians of the land in the locality.
26. See The Sierra Leone Local Government Act, 2004: Article 106 (2).
27. See Mohamed Massaquoi, "Sierra Leone: Opinion—Chieftaincy Reforms and the Role of Governance." Article appearing in the *Concord Times*, Freetown. March 18, 2009
28. This is the name given to both men and women appointed to the position to lead a village community of about 150–200 people.
29. This information obtained from the village head man in Waterloo, Western Rural Area.
30. See Barbara Pozzoni and Nalini Kumar. 2005. "A Review of the Literature on Participatory Approaches to Local Development for an Evaluation of the Effectiveness of the World Bank Support for Community-Based and Driven Development Approaches." *Operations Evaluation Department.* Washington, DC: The World Bank.
31. See Todd Moss, Gunilla Pettersson, and Nicholas van de Walle. 2006. "An Aid-Institution Paradox? A Review Essay on Aid Dependency and State Building in sub-Saharan Africa." In *Working Paper 74*. Washington, DC: Center for Global Development.

32. See Bryna Hallam, "Local Council not Involving Citizens, Study Finds," Article appearing in the Concord Times (Freetown) in November 2008.

33. Ibid.

34. Aruna Turay wrote this article under the title "In Sierra Leone, Vice President Sam-Sumana Dismayed over slow Decentralization." *Awareness Times* Newspapers, Freetown. June 1, 2009.

35. See Archibald, Steven and Paul Richards. 2002. "Converts to Human Rights? Popular Debates about war and Justice in Rural Central Sierra Leone." *Africa*. Vol. 72 (3). p. 339.

36. The Abidjan Peace Accord was one of the two major Peace Accords to end the conflict in Sierra Leone. It was signed on November 30, 1996 in Abidjan, Cote D'Ivoire.

37. The AFRC released Johnny Paul Koroma, who had earlier on been jailed for his involvement in the 1996 coup attempt to be the chairman and leader of the AFRC. The AFRC was ousted from office by the ECOMOG forces led by Nigerian troops, and Kabbah was restored to office from exile in Guinea.

38. See http://www.humanrightssl.org/newsite/index.htm and http://www.anticorruption.gov.sl.

39. Ibid.

40. Ibid.

41. This is stipulated in the Government of Sierra Leone's Justice Sector Reform Strategy and Investment Plan 2008–2010. This is 109-page document.

42. See Government of Sierra Leone: Justice sector Reform, 2007

43. Human Rights Watch, World Report 2007, Sierra Leone Entry, http://web.amnesty.org/library/index/engfr/510022006.

44. Institutional Reform and Capacity Building project, October 2007. http://ircbp.sl/drwebsite/uploads/nps-2007_report.pdf.

45. UNDP Advisory Note, Joint Missions for Crisis, Prevention and Recovery / Bureau for Development Policy Sept. 11–19, 2005; "Contributing to the Consolidation of Peace in Sierra Leone Through Support to Justice, Rule of Law and Human Rights."

46. Fairness for both victims and perpetrators and due process of the law is critical to ensure sustainable post-conflict environment.

47. See the Government of Sierra Leone: Justice Sector Reform. 2007: 19

48. Ibid. p. 20.

49. Ibid., p. 15

50. In the Krio language the title translate "afta we den arrest yu; wetin neks."

Chapter Four

Economic Reforms

This section of the book examines the economic outlook of post-conflict Sierra Leonean. It begins by navigating the economic argument for war onset. It further discusses the strategies that the government of Sierra Leone, its institutions, and society has undertaken to address domestic economic sustainability, job creation and job security, improvement in income levels, and the general economic well-being of the Sierra Leonean people. In analyzing the post-conflict Sierra Leonean economy, it is important not to ignore some of the provisions in the Abidjan (1996) and the Lome (1999) Peace Accords. These documents are critical to the consolidation of peace after the long and violent conflict in Sierra Leone; and especially in the Sierra Leonean case where, as a result of the multifaceted nature of the cause of conflict, a comprehensive strategy is needed to reform all aspects of the society, which includes the country's economy.

ECONOMIC ARGUMENT FOR ONSET OF CIVIL WAR

One of the reasons underlying the onset of civil conflicts is elites' economic marginalization of the rest of the population from the share of the nation's resources.[1] Others have taken the economic argument beyond the greed of political elite, and argued that civil wars also have their roots in world economy as a result of the intense global trade relationships between states.[2] Globalization has resulted in violence in certain types of states that possess raw materials that have high demand on the global market.[3] Again states that have experienced domestic wars have also had persistent economic declines.[4] States such as Liberia and Sierra Leone, which are mostly cited, had fundamental economic problems in the period leading to the internal conflicts. Individual incomes in particular and the gross domestic product (GDP) of these states in general consistently declined over the years leading to the onset of the civil war.[5]

The "greed and grievance" argument[6] is relevant in this instance regarding the extent to which individual economic insecurity could mutate and/or advance into a collective rallying point that could cut across ethnicities. Grievance, usually a bottom-up phenomenon, sheds more light on how consistent the exploitation and marginalization of a section of the population leads to a situation where these groups who fall below the law[7] and lose the protection of the law resort to heinous acts of violence.[8] Morgan Tsvangarai's call for a massive protest against the Mugabe government after the disputed 2008 presidential elections was largely ignored by a large section of the Zimbabwean population. This include those that supported Tsvangarai and who have secured for themselves jobs either in the public or private sector, or have well-established self-employments.[9] Such actions cannot be described as acts of cowardice, though the article cites fear as a major factor for the protest boycott. However, it highlights the extent to which personal and stable economic securities could be a disincentive to violent acts that could culminate in political instability and civil conflicts.

People's economic security, one of the important components of human security,[10] and which has also been identified in the UNDP human development report has positive impact on the overall domestic and world economies, and also in ensuring stable societies. World leaders struggled to deal with the recession that occurred in the third quarter of 2008 and well into 2009. Trillions of dollars in economic stimulus packages[11] were injected into the economies of states across the globe. The "ticking time bomb" scenario[12] was invoked by global leaders, and that the failure on the part of governments to inject massive amount of capital into their economies could eventually lead to an unprecedented global recession of greater magnitude not seen since the Great Depression. John Maynard Keynes seems to be winning the economic rescue argument. Keynesian economic models have become the "new normal" approach to tackling economic crisis. Even in pure capitalist states such as the United States, the government took control[13] of some banks and auto industries in 2009 and became co-owners amid protests from conservative groups who see such actions as government overreach and intrusion into the free market economy. The US government's intention, however, was to have control over the recession and to prevent massive unemployment. The role of the government in developing and ensuring strong economies that support job creation need not be underestimated, and in the case of Sierra Leone, in the post-conflict, the government's role in ensuring a healthy economy and creating jobs becomes very important.

When economic insecurities and severe income inequalities become triggers for internal conflict, economic security becomes a priority in states transitioning to a peaceful post-conflict reconstruction after a violent and prolonged conflict.[14] The essence of rationality and self-interest necessitates that the political elites make economic security a priority, since it is less costly and ensures a stable society and their own political survival. The government's role in stimulating the economy and moreso in Africa, becomes critical because the government is the only actor that has the resources or the means to raise those resources necessary to boost the economy. In most of these post-conflict states, the government becomes the sole legitimate entity to embark on the responsibility to jump-start the economy, at least in the short term.

THE ABIDJAN AND LOME PEACE ACCORDS

The peace negotiations that culminated in the 1996 Abidjan Peace Accord had well-represented third parties or guarantors. Parties to the peace negotiation included the belligerents (Ahmed Tejan Kabbah and Foday Sankoh), the then Ivorian president, Konan Bedie, and the special envoy of the UN Secretary-General for Sierra Leone. Others included representatives from the African Union and the commonwealth which were present and signatories to the peace accord. The twenty-eight provisions contained in the Abidjan Peace Accord signed in November 1996, is one of the most comprehensive documents to end the conflict in Sierra Leone.

The provisions under Articles 26 and 27 of the Abidjan Peace Accord noted some critical socio-economic problems that brought about the onset of the war, and set forth strategies to address these problems during the post-conflict recovery. Critical among these issues were:

- The enhancement of the nation's productive capacity by involving fully the grassroots in the reconstruction and development process.
- The creation of equal opportunities and access to the country's resources for all Sierra Leoneans, both in the rural and the urban areas.
- The recognition and importance of education in enhancing human capacity in the recovery process. Free and compulsory education was to be made available at the basic level.
- The provision of sustainable job opportunities for the Sierra Leonean people, especially the youth.
- The promotion of a sustainable rural development program by making agriculture the engine of the recovery process.

These provisions focus on the Sierra Leonean people, including the youth, regarding how best to enhance human capacities and create job opportunities needed for sustainable post-conflict recovery. Capacity building is therefore significant to achieve a sustainable economic health in the post-conflict.

Again, making the youth issue the center of post-conflict economic recovery is a prudent idea. Unlike other sub-Saharan African states where the youth (15–34 years of age) constitutes about 34 percent of the population, in the Sierra Leonean case, the youth constitutes 60 percent of the population. What makes the enhancement of the human resource capacity of the youth central in any strategy to create a strong post-conflict economic recovery in Sierra Leone is the fact that not only does that category represent a higher percentage of the population, but also the youth were mostly the ones that were recruited to fight in the violent war. The conflict became lucrative to the youth because it met their economic needs in terms of receiving income[15] for their services as fighters, as well as having the arms to defend themselves which guarantees their own personal survival. The youth issue could therefore be the Achilles' heel of any sustainable strategy in post-conflict Sierra Leone.

The 1999 Lome Peace Accord, however, did not make provisions regarding how the economic needs of the Sierra Leonean people would be met in terms of ensuring sustainable cash flow for families who need that stability at the basic level for survival and enhancement of economic well-being. The peace accord dealt with the bigger issues of disarmament and peace. However, Article VII comprehensively addressed how to manage the country's strategic resources in the reconstruction and development process. It expanded the government's sole control of the nation's natural resources by entrusting to the government of Sierra Leone the power to exploit and export gold, diamonds, and other natural resources. This provision establishes an enclave economy that has impeded development, the economic history of the country seems to suggest. The conflict in Sierra Leone and other places like Angola could also be seen as conflict for the control of mineral and other natural resources.[16] There is also the likelihood that government control of these natural resources could open the way for endemic corruption where government officials use their influential positions to reward themselves and their political cronies with the nation's resources. The thirty-seven articles in the Lome Peace Accord did not mention any development in the agriculture sector. Again, making the agriculture sector the engine for growth in the post-conflict recovery as stipulated in the 1996 Abidjan Peace Accord has not been realized yet. Vast amount of arable land for agriculture in Sierra Leone currently lay idle and not exploited.

DEMOBILIZATION, DISARMAMENT, AND REINTEGRATION (DDR) PROGRAM

Several provisions of the 1996 Abidjan and the 1999 Lome Peace Accords recognize the importance of retraining of ex-combatants to equip them with appropriate skills in order for them to secure appropriate jobs and to meet their economic needs. The DDR program trained ex-combatants in skills of their choice. After giving the ex-combatants the entrepreneurial know-how to enhance their human capacity and to assist them in establishing their own businesses, many of the trainees were given start-up kits including tools and other machinery and some finance capital.

Sierra Leoneans who did not take part in the civil war have criticized the DDR program for not being comprehensive enough. They argue that the program targeted and favored only the ex-combatants who broke the law, maimed, and killed their fellow citizens to the detriment of those who were law-abiding and are still jobless after the war.[17] Embittered Sierra Leoneans, as featured in a National Geographic documentary, view the DDR program as more of an appeasement program on the part of the government and international stakeholders, noting that it could be more of a motivating factor for future unrest than a strategy to forestall such occurrences.

The extent to which the DDR program fits into the overall sustainable post-conflict economic development of Sierra Leone is a pivotal issue in the post-conflict economic puzzle. There is no doubt Sierra Leone is rich in natural resources, including diamonds, which were also at the epicenter of the conflict. The Sierra Leonean government currently is in control, and manages its natural resources. However, equally vital sectors of the economy, such as agriculture, have been neglected by the government. Sierra Leone exports cash crops like cocoa and coffee but the country's import bills include substantial food importation. According to data collected by the Statistical Services (Statistics, Sierra Leone), out of the 10,840 total number of establishments identified in 2005, only 52 are involved in agriculture, forestry, and fishing.[18] What is troubling with this statistics is the fact that the government has failed to take advantage of the availability of a vast expanse of arable land available and to tailor the DDR program toward the agriculture sector; compared to the other sectors, the agriculture sector in Sierra Leone has enormous prospects.

However, some ex-combatants that completed the skill and other training programs were instead given motorbikes to use as "Okadas"[19] to generate income; some were also given handy-man tools and other equipments to establish their own businesses. There are reports that quite a number of these ex-combatant trainees have sold their motorbikes and tools and are back to idle lifestyles in the Freetown area and other provincial capitals such as Bo, Makeni, and Kenema. This is a serious threat to human security. The Sierra Leonean government has not been able to garner enough will to make the agriculture sector attractive and also a priority in order to rein in the idle human resource and channel it to more sustainable development[20] ventures.

HUMAN RESOURCE MANAGEMENT AND CAPACITY BUILDING

Education, both formal and informal, has been one of the essential areas that the government of Sierra Leone is focusing on in its broad document "Vision 2025"[21] unveiled in August 2003. Before this date, the government had already introduced, in 2001, a free and compulsory primary education (from grades 1–6) in all public schools throughout the country. The UNDP's 2002 statistical report indicated that the literacy rate in Sierra Leone held study in the period 1994–1998 at 30 percent. The 2004 literacy rate was 35.1 percent and it is currently around 38 percent. The government, however, has focused much attention on informal education by organizing numerous and regular basic skill workshops throughout the provinces to as many adults as possible who need such training to enable them to engage in some form of sustainable economic activities.

POLITICAL PARTIES AND CAPACITY BUILDING

All stakeholders within Sierra Leone have seized on this broad initiative of human capacity building, as outlined in the "Vision 2025" government document, to design programs to achieve this goal. For instance, political parties in the minority have been very active and have taken advantage of the capacity-building objective to attract voters to their camps. The ruling All People's Congress (APC) has also been very active on issues of capacity building. In an interview with the APC youth director in Makeni, capital of the Northern Province, one of the modus operandi of the ruling APC Party is to use the youth wing to constantly engage the youth by organizing youth employment workshops that give priority to agriculture as a means to enhance the human capacity of these youths. Furthermore, the APC youth wing has also been instrumental in the transformation of ghettos in urban areas by building vocational centers at these deplorable locations. The group has also advocated for the establishment of numerous vocational institutes throughout the chiefdoms. The government has backed its youth wing with a lot of resources in order to achieve its goal of mobilizing the youth to embark on some decent economic activities besides organizing them for political purposes.

The Sierra Leone People's Party (SLPP), which was the government in power before the 2007 elections, was very instrumental in establishing government agencies that helped promote a more sustainable human capacity building. Partnered with the World Bank, United Nations, the Islamic Development Bank, African Development Bank, the German government, and other external financiers, the SLPP government established the National Commission for Social Action (NaCSA). This organization is primarily responsible for funding community-based and demand-driven activities with the objective of reducing or eliminating poverty within the communities.[22] NaCSA has been involved in community development projects such as the construction of homes for displaced people. This has resulted in stronger communities and increased income for the communities through the wages the people receive for working at construction sites. NaCSA is also instrumental in the establishment of micro-finance houses that extend start-up capital to new entrepreneurs venturing into the business arena. Though the SLPP is currently not the party in control of the government, its youth wing is relentless on the goal of organizing activities that enhance the economic independence of the youth in Sierra Leone.

A third political party, the People's Movement for Democratic Change (PMDC), a break-away political party from the SLPP, has devoted its daily meetings[23] to challenging the youth to embark on agricultural activities in order to ensure food security for Sierra Leone instead of having to rely on donors for food. This is a new party with very limited resources to carry out this difficult task of challenging the youth to engage in agricultural activities. However, the goal is laudable and in the right direction.

Organizing youth employment workshops is a common practice in Sierra Leone. It is, however, not clear what the correlation is between these workshops and the level of employment. Is it the case that the youth show up at such workshops just to take advantage of the breakfast and lunches that are served, or are seriously interested in building their human capacities? These are legitimate concerns since the numerous workshops do not seem to have much effect in reducing the number of the youth congregating around street corners in major cities across the provinces. Another concern may be the extent to which youth employment strategies are being evaluated to ascertain the effect on employment. Finally, serious studies have to be done regarding what innovative and remedial strategies are being put in place by the government to make the agriculture sector an attractive sector to the youth?

INTERNATIONAL AND LOCAL NGOS

International non-governmental organizations (NGOs) such as the Global Rescue Mission (GRM) are also involved in organizing employment workshops. GRM has organized several of these workshops, especially for women, to enhance their human capacity and to prepare them for the job market. Gender-sensitive programs have moved to the forefront development strategies. With women comprising about 52 percent of the Sierra Leonean population and occupying a larger percentage of the catchment economic space (farming, trading, etc.) it is imperative that much resources be spent on programs that positively impact their lives. In some instances, GRM has partnered with community-based organizations (CBOs) such as the Kenema Youth Alliance (KYA) in the Eastern Province to organize training workshops. Such partnerships help to bridge the gap between the culture of the community with the foreign cultural imports and innovations in dealing with the contemporary reality and challenges that Sierra Leonean communities face—a key element of sustainable development. Action Aid, an international NGO, which has transformed itself into a local/international NGO in Sierra Leone, has long been involved in youth job training and employment. For instance, Action Aid is involved in the Stabilizing Export (STABEX) project, a rice farm project with the objective of enhancing employment opportunities and more broadly, to reduce the country's reliance on the importation of rice from abroad.

However, the rift between local and international NGOs, and between the local NGOs themselves, cannot be overemphasized. International NGOs are competing with the local NGOs for project space in the country. Funding has been a major challenge to the operations of local NGOs. Local NGOs have not been successful in securing donor funding due to the lack of credible financial reports to substantiate their application for external funding. Secondly, the downturn in the global economy is not favorable to the effort at securing funds from foreign sources. Consequently, local NGOs mostly rely on the international NGOs operating in Sierra Leone to "sub-lease" funds to support their activities because the international NGOs have the credibility and reliable external funding sources. The ideal strategy probably would have been for the international NGOs to partner with the local NGOs who best understand the culture and needs of the local people in order to deliver sustainable projects to the communities, instead of competing with them. However, due to an extremely large number of local NGOs, there is a lot of pressure on the international NGOs regarding who and what project to select. With much pressure on the local NGOs, some have resorted to undercutting their contemporaries to gain favorability and funding advantage.[24] This jeopardizes the chances of other NGOs to obtain funding. Thus, the role of NGOs in the reconstruction effort seems to be counter-productive to the main recovery objective. There are instances where local NGOs have refused to attend funding meetings with their international NGO partners out of concern that their competitors (other local NGOs) would "steal" their business plans and undercut them.[25]

In other cases, especially in the rural area of Freetown, the community in the Waterloo area has expressed concern that international NGOs have not supported trainees with start-up kits and other equipment.[26] The resources spent in training the people go waste because of the lack of equipment to start business; this renders these projects unsustainable. Still in the Waterloo area there are concerns that while participants are trained in agricultural skills, agriculture is still at the subsistence level, mostly due to the fact that the equipment that is needed for mid-level mechanized farming are simply not provided.

DISTRICT AND LOCAL COUNCIL

District and local councils have also been involved in the drive to enhance capacity building. For instance, in the western rural (Waterloo) area, the local council has organized series of employment training in skills such as soap-making, tie and dye, carpentry, masonry, and gardening. The district assemblies, on the other hand, have used some monies from the Devolved Fund[27] to organize job training and also create jobs.

LOCAL NGOS AND JOB CREATION

The ubiquitous presence of local NGOs, and the extent to which they have placed themselves in the center of job creation and economic empowerment within the Sierra Leonean society, cannot be overemphasized. In cities both large and small, the existence and presence of NGOs is felt in every street corner. Some Sierra Leoneans have even come to believe that the local NGOs are a major part of the private sector initiative that the government is promoting, since they are the organizations that people see providing some form of employment to the youth. However, local NGOs are at the mercy of locally based international NGOs and compete with them for donor funds. Because it is difficult to substantiate the credibility of local NGOs, the foreign NGOs are more successful in securing donor funds than the local NGOs. This has affected the ability of local NGOs to expand their operations. Local NGOs have to wait for longer periods of time (some for about two years) to get approval for donor funds and support to undertake their projects.[28]

Since NGOs do not generate funds from their activities, their ability to provide employment opportunities is impeded by the lack of available funds from foreign donors. They are, therefore, not able to provide sustainable employment opportunities. Those local NGOs that are able to provide jobs year round do so by paying meager wages to their employees.

NATIONAL SOCIAL SECURITY AND INSURANCE TRUST (NASSIT)

In July 2001, the Sierra Leonean government established NASSIT,[29] as a statutory public trust to administer the country's pension scheme. Like many countries, both developed and underdeveloped, social security insurance serves as an economic safety net that provides regular financial payments to retirees after they have contributed to the scheme and reached an established retirement age. In Sierra Leone, to qualify for social security, an individual should be at the age of 60 and should have contributed to the scheme for at least fifteen years. Those who elect to retire at an earlier age could do so and receive a reduced pension. NASSIT also makes provisions for an invalidity pension; those individuals who become incapacitated on the job, and survivors of employees who qualify for the pension scheme, are compensated.

With a 40–45 percent unemployment rate in the country, and most of those falling into the category of unemployed youth (some of them ex-combatants), this economic safety net may not achieve the intended goal in the short and medium term. In the long term, however, and with the hope that the economy improves and the youth find work, they can contribute to the scheme which will make it a viable project. Sudden outbursts of violence and crimes that sometimes have no probable cause, and that mostly involve the youth, requires a much more pragmatic strategy to deal with the short- and medium-term economic and other social safety nets in order to consolidate the seemingly fragile peace in the country. The current situation poses grave human security problems and makes the fragile political environment even more vulnerable. Apart from the unemployed youth that has been the main focus, there are those who are in the informal sector and do not contribute to the scheme. This category of people would not benefit from the pension scheme when they reach old age, and at a time that they would need such safety nets the most.

SIERRA LEONE CHAMBER OF COMMERCE

The push to establish a sustainable economic environment in Sierra Leone put the Sierra Leone Chamber of Commerce, Industry and Agriculture at the center of the discourse of economic security in Sierra Leone. The Sierra Leone Chamber of Commerce is an organization that serves as a hub for organizing the private sector and to enhance the private sector's role in the post-conflict economic recovery. The goals of the Chamber of Commerce include the dissemination of information to its members regarding opportunities for partnerships with foreign businesses. They also provide information on how small businesses could pool capital together to establish medium, and possibly larger and efficient firms in order to achieve leverage in negotiating credit, import and export trade negotiations. The Chamber also provides information on how businesses can network and assist each other to achieve their overall business goals.

Since its establishment in 1961 the Chamber of Commerce has actively engaged the government of Sierra Leone with regard to laws that ensure a strong private sector participation in the economy and the consequent effect on economic development. It has been very instrumental in the reduction or elimination of regulatory barriers to investments and prohibitive and unproductive tax laws in the country.

The Chamber, however, has not been able to make headway with the government regarding an investment code schedule that creates incentives for private businesses to venture into the agriculture sector. This has resulted in a huge disincentive for private businesses to invest in the agricultural sector.[30]

Still, there are major infrastructural bottlenecks that hinder the full potentials of the Chamber of Commerce's role in assisting private businesses in the post-conflict economic recovery. While the government of Sierra Leone has embarked on massive road networks, it is more concentrated in linking the major cities to the capital, Freetown. There are not enough road networks to link the rural areas with major cities and the nation's capital in order to open those places to investments in agriculture. Investment in road networks is a critical part of the reconstruction process, especially when most people live in the rural areas and agriculture and mineral sectors continue to be a critical part of the Sierra Leonean economy. Agriculture, for instance, accounts for about 58.5 percent of the GDP; while diamond mining exports remain the highest foreign exchange earner, bringing in about US$ 250–300 million annually.

A statistical document on agriculture by the government of Sierra Leone and collaborated by the United Nations Population Fund (UNPFA) and the European Union (EU) indicates that Sierra Leone has about 5.4 million hectares of potential land suitable for agriculture. This is about 74 percent of the total land area of the country.[31] However, only 34 percent of the arable land is cultivated. The statistics also show that there are more women (51 percent) than men (49 percent) engaged in the agriculture sector. Most of the men, especially the youth are in the big cities (Freetown, Kenema, Makeni, and Bo) with no work to do. Not only is this a serious threat to food security, it also threatens human security in terms of the dangers and potential for youth exploitation and instability. Disgruntled political elites and others who do not want to use the political process to resolve society problems could hire the services of unemployed and aggrieved youth for their own personal gains.

Apart from the infrastructural challenges that impede the ability of the Chamber of Commerce to mobilize and revitalize the private sector in the developmental effort, there is also the energy problem. Intermittent and sometimes non-existent electricity supply is a major problem not only for industries in the private sector, but also for the government in meeting the challenges of the speed of globalization regarding the receiving and dissemination of information. The completion of the Bumbuna hydroelectric project, situated on the Rokel River to generate electricity, is a step in the right direction. It could provide electricity that is needed for the establishment of agro-based industries.

On a more positive note, there is a vibrant telecommunication (cell phone) industry that is linking Freetown with the rest of the provinces. Businesses and individuals can now have easy and reliable access to their business partners and relations respectively than was hitherto the case. The telecommunication sector has created employment opportunities for some sections of the Sierra Leonean population. People with little capital are involved in the business of buying and selling of phone card units. However, it is not clear the extent to which the increase in cell phone use translates into effective and sustainable economic development. This is because not only are the cell phone units expensive, but also most people using cell phones are unemployed and usually make calls to friends and other relations that have no direct economic effect.

THE YOUTH QUESTION

Most of the combatants in Sierra Leone's eleven-year civil conflict were youth with ages ranging between 15–35 years. It is estimated that 55–60 percent of the 5.4 million people in Sierra Leone are within the youth population. Any attempt to forestall future youth involvement in conflict must address the "youth question"[32] and their involvement in the post-conflict developmental process, as well as providing them with opportunities to enhance their economic security. Providing sustainable employment opportunities for the youth is a major concern for policymakers and other stakeholders.

After the war was declared ended in January 2002, the then president, Tejan Kabbah, launched a National Youth Policy in June 2002 to engage the youth in the post-conflict development process. The target of the policy included the revitalization of the Ministry of Youth and Sports and to develop strategies that would ensure accelerated development in the economic, social, and the psychological life of the youth.[33] In addition to that, the policy aimed to re-sensitize the youth by instilling in them the right productive mind-set to get them to understand how critical their mental and physical abilities are to the development of the country, and not to use their human abilities and resources to destroy their fellow citizens and ruin their country's infrastructure and resources.[34] In light of this, the Ministry of Youth and Sports was to collaborate with and encourage other public sector ministries and the private sector to provide employment to the youth. Other donor organizations such as the UNDP, UNICEF, WHO, and the UNFPA were also involved in activities and workshops to address youth unemployment in the country. Creating descent and sustainable employment for the youth is critical, in that many of the youth who were involved in the war considered themselves employed at the time. They had "regular income" (though meager) for their services as rebel combatants, and also profited from the booty obtained through looting of homes, villages, mineral sites, and government facilities.

The government's strategy for a comprehensive national youth policy was to create job opportunities, provide skills training, information and sensitization outreach, institute community based development, establish a presidential award for excellence, and encourage youth consultation and participation in their various communities and in other public and governmental services. To help decentralize the policy, and to make sure no youth is left behind, district youth committees were set up to identify the youth in the district and to involve them in the planning, organizing, and implementation of programs within the districts.

The national youth policy also included responsibilities for the parents. Parents were charged with guiding their youth, especially those within the ages of 15–18 years, to discover their potentials and create the enabling environment for them to develop those potentials. Education was made the responsibility of the parents; parents are to ensure that their children take advantage of the educational opportunities the government has provided. The youth, in the national youth policy, were also charged with the responsibility of adhering to their utmost civic responsibilities, develop their potential talents, and embrace peace, security, and developmental goals.

A comprehensive youth policy, as outlined in the national youth policy, has its own challenges, especially in after-conflict situations where resources are in limited supply and everyone wants their deplorable situations to be turned around quickly instead of having to make sacrifices in the recovery process. Some of these challenges include the commitment on the part of both the government and the youth to the youth policy. On the youth side, it has to do with the necessary motivations and whether or not such motivations and incentives will enable them to see the light at the end of the tunnel and fully commit themselves to the policy. On the government side, the challenge is the political will to get this policy through by making it a priority. The state's resources may pose a challenge; but prioritizing the issue that concerns the youth as stated in the youth policy will move the recovery further along. There are currently numerous projects in Sierra Leone to help the country rebuild and recover from the devastating conflict. Various stakeholders have had the opportunity to contribute and to assist the country to rebuild. Still, questions remain regarding how the youth would take advantage of these resources to enhance their economic security to aid in ensuring a sustainable post-conflict Sierra Leone.

The youth question has been a great concern to stakeholders—both local and international governments—as well as donors. The general consensus regarding the youth in Sierra Leone is that the most important threat to human security is the lack of employment opportunities for the youth. Employment workshops and skills training, coupled with direct donor involvement to foster capacity building and assist the youth since 2002 have not produce the intended outcome. Youth unemployment has been dubbed the "ticking time bomb" by many analysts[35] and the youth[36] themselves. Youth unemployment has consistently led to the development of gang activities, cultism, and youth violence—a major threat to post-conflict peace consolidation. There are also cases where youth unemployment has sour relationships between students at the different universities in the country that goes all the way to the arena of public office; subsequently, alumni protect public jobs for those from their alma mater.

The change in government at the end of 2007, no doubt, was a referendum on the Sierra Leone People's Party (SLPP) government's inability to provide jobs for the youth. The All People's Congress (APC) party capitalized on the youth unemployment situation and convinced the youth to overwhelmingly vote for the party. This is an indication that the youth, at least, are aware of the issues that are important to them. However, the current APC party in government has not been able to deliver the jobs either. In August 2007, for instance, the UN estimated that the unemployment rate in Sierra Leone is 65 percent.[37] It is not difficult, on a first time visit to the country, to notice problem of youth unemployment in the country. The youth could be seen loitering from one side of the street to the other in the big cities such as Freetown, Makeni, Kenema, Kono, Tongo, and Bo, where they have relocated after the war. Those that want to stay out of trouble spend most of their idle time watching soccer channels such as the English Premier League.

Some have remarked that the Sierra Leone political elites actually favor the status quo of high youth since they exploit the situation by using the idle youth to terrorize their political opponents during election time.[38] She noted that political elites provide money, drugs, and alcohol to the idle youth so they can unleash terror on their political opponents in places such as Kailahun, Bo, and Kenema in July and August of 2007. In addition, areas such as Kono, Freetown, Tongo, and Port Lokko also experienced such violence in 2008.

At best, political elites' promises of job creation are basically the transfer of existing public jobs from supporters of the past government to supporters of the new government. The patronage system is very well entrenched in the politics and society of Sierra Leone. This makes both the election and after-election environment extremely uncomfortable times for those that have jobs in the public sector. The reality is that a large number of people lose jobs in the public sector in the aftermath of elections when there is a change in government. Consequently, the job creation is basically an "elimination by substitution" strategy where the new government removes hardworking and experienced individuals occupying existing positions in the public sector, and replaces them with its supporters and cronies. This creates the tendency for existing governments to use whatever means possible to stay in office to ensure economic stability for its supporters. Though this situation is not unique to Sierra Leone, the situation is critical because people vote along regional lines. Northerners votes for candidates from the north, and southeasterners also vote for their ethnic candidates. Thus, any changes in government literally mean the marginalization of particular provinces and ethnicities. It is clear that the marginalization of certain ethnic groups has become structural within the Sierra Leonean societies just like it exists in other Third World countries. Marginalization correlates with change of government. This is a very serious concern and impacts human security negatively. Unpredictability, apprehension and instability, and sudden behavioral attitudes are likely consequences of such phenomenon. Government's ability to overcome this hurdle is critical for sustainable after-conflict peace. Transferring the letter in the youth policy to realized goals is non-negotiable.

ECONOMIC SECURITY AND SUSTAINABLE DEVELOPMENT IN POST-CONFLICT SIERRA LEONE

Creating employment opportunities to ensure economic security is a daunting challenge even for some developed states. For post-conflict states the situation becomes even more precarious. The discussion shows the tremendous efforts at the governmental, donor, and local levels to create employment opportunities for the Sierra Leonean people. Most Sierra Leoneans acknowledge the fact that the government is making all the effort to create employment. The reason why job creation policies have not realized the intended goals and why the unemployment rate continues to rise need to be examined. Clearly, there is a gap between the structural realities of the country and the effectiveness of government job-creating policies.

There is currently a mismatch of labor and resources in the country. Whereas the rural areas need the labor of the youth to engage in agricultural activities, most of the youth have relocated to the big cities. In the big cities one needs substantial finance capital to be able to begin some commercial activities in order to improve their economic and living conditions. The youth do not have access to such finances. Economic securities have continually worsened for many people in Sierra Leone. The challenge is for the government to turn the situation around. Sierra Leone has 65 percent of its arable land not exploited. The government needs to take the initiative to engage in agriculture and make it attractive by establishing small- , medium- , or large-scale mechanized farming ventures and provide the appropriate incentives and motivations to attract the youth that have relocated to the urban areas to be partners in the initiative. Eventually, the government can withdraw from active involvement in these agricultural projects and turn it over to private hands. This is a challenging endeavor. In the short term, however, sustainable employment would be achieved and idle hands would be kept busy. It is the prerogative of the government as to whether or not the unemployment situation threatens national security and development, and what pragmatic steps need to be taken in order to ensure a reduction of the unemployment rate. Elites have to answer the question as to whether or not the status quo is acceptable. Obviously, if the causes of the conflict in Sierra Leone provide any lessons to the political elites, then commitment to economic security will be a priority. It is also rational to pursue such a goal since in the long run, both elites and the people benefit. The current unemployment situation in Sierra Leone threatens human security and it is a drag on the post-conflict reconstruction and recovery.

NOTES

1. See Mats Berdal and David M. Malone (eds.) 2000. *Greed and Grievance: Economic Agendas in Civil Wars.* Boulder, CO: Lynne Reinner Publishers, Inc. Also, David Keen. 2000. "Incentives and Disincentives for Violence" In *Greed and Grievance: Economic Agendas in Civil Wars.* Mats Berdal and David M. Malone (eds.) Boulder, CO: Lynne Reinner Publishers, Inc.

2. See William Reno. 2000. "Shadow States and the Political Economy of Civil Wars" In *Greed and Grievance: Economic Agendas in Civil Wars.* Mats Berdal and David M. Malone (eds.) Boulder, CO: Lynne Reinner Publishers, Inc.

3. Ibid.

4. See Paul Collier and Anke Hoeffler. 2000. *Greed and Grievance in Civil Wars.* Washington, DC: World Bank Development Research Group. Also, Paul Collier, Anke Hoeffler, and Dominic Rohner. 2006. "Beyond Greed and Grievance: Feasibility and Civil War," *Center for the Study of African Economies,* Working Paper. 10 (7) August, 2006.

5. See Paul Collier and Nicholas Sambanis (eds.) 2005. *Understanding Civil War (Volume 1: Africa): Evidence and Analysis.* Washington, DC: The World Bank, pp. 305–96. Also, James D. Fearon and David D. Laitin. "Ethnicity, Insurgency, and Civil War" *American Political Science Review* 97, 1 (Feb 2003): pp.75–79

6. This is championed by Paul Collier in his attempt to explain the onset of civil conflict.

7. Marginalized individuals fall below the protection of the law due to the lack of resources (financial and/or information) necessary to fully engage the legal system to their advantage.

8. David Keen. 2000. "Incentives and Disincentives for Violence." In *Greed and Grievance: Economic Agendas in Civil Wars.* Mats Berdal and David M. Malone (eds.) Boulder, CO: Lynne Reinner Publishers, Inc.

9. See Voice of America online article in April 2008. "Opposition Strike falters in Zimbabwe" http://www1.voanews.com/english/news/a-13-2008-04-15-voa61-66747377.html.

10. See Agostinho Zacarias. 2003. "Redefining Security." In *From Cape to Congo: Southern Africa's Evolving Security Challenges.* Mwesiga Baregu and Christopher Landsberg (eds.) Boulder, CO: Lynne Rienner Publishers, Inc., p. 43.

11. Even including China.

12. The possibility of massive and sudden catastrophe occurring.

13. In the United States, most of the US government's investments in banks and the auto industries have been paid with interest. Taxpayers monies, have therefore been recouped.

14. See Paul Collier and Nicholas Sambanis (eds.) 2005. *Understanding Civil War (Volume 1: Africa): Evidence and Analysis.* Washington: The World Bank.

15. This could be both cash and in-kind from looted booty.

16. See Paul Richards. 1996. *Fighting for the Rain Forest: War, Youth and Resources in Sierra Leone.* London: Villiers Publications.

17. See excerpts from a National Geographic documentary titled, "Blood Money."

18. The breakdown is as follows: crop farming, 4; livestock farming, 6; poultry farming, 3; forestry, 6; fishing, 33.

19. Okadas are motorbikes used as taxis to transport people from one spot (mostly in the urban and some rural areas) to their destinations for a fee.

20. This is contained in the booklet put together for the Sierra Leone Chamber of Commerce, Industry and Agriculture, 45th Anniversary Dinner held at the Bank of Sierra Leone Complex, Kingtom, Freetown, on December 13, 2006. p. 15.

21. See http://unipsil.unmissions.org/portals/unipsil/media/publications/Vision_2025.pdf.

22. NaCSA was established in November 2001 as a "Social Fund" by an Act of Parliament. http://www.nacsasl.org/index.html.

23. This was the information I received from the leadership when I participated in one of their meetings on a research trip.

24. Information obtained from interview with a CEO of one of the local NGOs in Freetown, Sierra Leone. Some are even afraid that others will "steal" their business plans and thus do not want to undertake any collaborative ventures with each other.

25. Ibid.

26. Information received from the Village Headman in the Waterloo area in Rural Freetown.

27. Devolved fund is the allocation from the Central government of Sierra Leone to the respective districts to supplement their budget and also embark on developmental projects.

28. This information was obtained from the CEO of CORD/SL; CORD/SL was the host organization during my research trip to Sierra Leone in the summer of 2009.

29. NASSIT was established in July 2001. http://www.daco-sl.org/encyclopedia/1_gov/1_3nassit.htm.

30. This is contained in the booklet put together for the Sierra Leone Chamber of Commerce, Industry and Agriculture, 45th Anniversary Dinner held at the Bank of Sierra Leone Complex, Kingtom, Freetown, on December 13, 2006. p. 15.

31. See the Government of Sierra Leone document "2004 Population and Housing Census: Analytical Report on Agriculture" by Bernadette Lahai (PhD), Ibrahim J. Sannoh, and Sheikh I. Koroma. p. viii.

32. In Sierra Leone, the term "Youth question" has come to be associated with what to do with the high unemployment rate among the youth population as well as the challenges this pose to the security and stability of the country.

33. See the 2002 Sierra Leone Youth Policy

34. Sierra Leone National Youth Policy, 2002: 3–4

35. Mariama Kandeh wrote an article "Sierra Leone: Youth's Unemployment: A Time Bomb" in the *Freetown Concord Times* on July 1, 2008.

36. This seems to be the general feelings of some youths interviewed in Freetown and the other provinces in Sierra Leone.

37. See Sierra Leone: Election Campaign focuses on the youth. http://allafrica.com/stories/200708080708.html.

38. See Mariama Kandeh, "Sierra Leone: Youth Unemployment: A Time Bomb." Article appearing in the *Concord Times* (Freetown) in July 1, 2008.

Chapter Five

Personal Security Reforms

Personal security protections are fundamental in the post-conflict. For a country such as Sierra Leone that had gone through civil conflict for eleven years, the people have to have the utmost assurance that the environment ensures safety in their persons. Thus they can walk outside at reasonable times of the day without the fear of any harm, and during the night they can sleep without the thought of any surprising attack on their homes. Achieving this end will send a signal of a new era in the country. This chapter discusses security reforms that could reduce concerns about personal security issues. It examines security reforms the Sierra Leonean government has put in place, and also efforts by civil society organizations, local and international NGOs in this direction.

PERSONAL SECURITY REFORMS

Deteriorating personal security situations not only spark domestic security problems but also result in severe regional and global insecurities.[1] Consequently, domestic insecurities have led to states having to deal with internally displaced persons (IDPs), refugee problems within the region, and xenophobic attitudes, both within states, the region, and across the globe. It is for these reasons that the UN, through its Human Rights Commission and other international non-governmental organizations such as Amnesty International, act as advocates and watchdogs for personal security to ensure people are safe in their own persons wherever they are. Franklin Delano Roosevelt described four types of freedom[2] in his address to the 77th US Congress in January of 1941. He emphasized that security should be provided to those that need it. These freedoms have become even more relevant in contemporary times, especially to people in states such as Sierra Leone that are recovering from prolonged conflict.

The period before and during the civil conflict witnessed deteriorating personal security problems in Sierra Leone. Civil and law-abiding Sierra Leoneans also suffered physical attacks and were gravely wounded. This resulted in permanent disabilities, prominent among them being the loss of limbs. Many, including women and children lost their lives, prematurely. In addition to that, several other Sierra Leoneans fled into the bush or migrated as refugees to neighboring states such as Guinea. Experiences like these leave an entire generation with bitter psychological memories. The effect may include the lack of trust between people in the communities in particular, and the government in general. In addition to these negative social effects, there could also be political and economic ramifications. Politically, it is possible for people to resent efforts at creating a political system that is fair and ensures safety. Some questions may include how different will the new system be from the old one? What appropriate safeguards need to be in place to ensure a sustainable system? Such questions call for serious reexamination of the societal values alongside its governance system, and whether or not the burden of a new political system is worth bearing. Likewise, decisions regarding long-term domestic investment such as owning land, building, and operating a business will be negatively affected. Foreign investors will also want to ensure that the post-conflict environment is safe enough to guarantee the security of their investments. The Sierra Leonean government needs to assure the people that it is in control of the country's institutions and resources in order to gain the confidence of the people. A secured society is fundamental to development.

THE ABIDJAN AND LOME PEACE ACCORDS

The Abidjan and the Lome Peace Accords are relevant to any structured security strategy in the after-conflict environment in Sierra Leone. The Peace Accords established a framework for which both parties to the conflict and the Sierra Leone people could reference regarding a new security strategy in the post-conflict. Articles 5 through 7 of the Abidjan Peace Accord, reemphasized in the Lome Peace Accord, stated clearly how to manage the rebels or ex-combatants. After a tumultuous period,[3] interspersed with the deployment of British troops to deal with the intermittent deteriorating security situations and other ceasefire agreements signed in Abuja, Nigeria, the Disarmament, Demobilization, and Reintegration (DDR) program was implemented. Deadly weapons, particularly small arms, were to be collected at a designated location (Assembly Zone). To make it more attractive for the ex-combatants to surrender such weapons and resurface from their hide-outs in the bush, the ex-combatants were to benefit from an amnesty for the heinous crimes they committed during the civil war. No criminal charges and other judicial actions were to be taken against any member of the Revolutionary United Front (RUF). Specialized security programs and activities were organized to ensure a smooth transition to resettle and reintegrate the combatants into communities that they originated and are known by members of that community.

In addition to resettling ex-combatants, both peace accords also provided for renegade soldiers to return to military barracks, thereby leaving only few Sierra Leonean army personnel to patrol the streets. The Sierra Leonean military was also to be downsized after the government had considered the appropriate level of personnel needed to meet security needs. Article 18(4) of the Lome Peace Accord also stipulates the withdrawal of all mercenaries from Sierra Leone[4] with immediate effect. Cleaning out the Sierra Leonean military was a very important piece of the post-conflict security puzzle. During the war, there were reports that some members of the military doubled as both regular and rebel soldiers. Those double agents were seen as regular soldiers who fought for the government during the day, and switched sides to fight alongside Forday Sankoh and the other rebels at night, earning themselves the name sobels.[5]

One of the major provisions of the Peace Accords was to retrain, strengthen, and resourcefully equip the Sierra Leone Police (SLP) to be effective in ensuring domestic security, and to help enforce the rule of law. Professionalism is to be the ethic of the Sierra Leonean police so that the service could regain the trust of the Sierra Leonean people. Other provisions in the Peace Accords stipulate adequate education and training, and the insulation of the Sierra Leone Police from any political trappings, thereby establishing an efficient and effective police service in post-conflict Sierra Leone.

The Sierra Leonean Police (SLP) not only has a history as a "litany of oppressive policing, nepotism, and corruption,"[6] but the act of corruption also permeates in the recruitment process by the appointment of friends and colleagues into the SLP. This has resulted in the lack of skill and high illiteracy within the police service.[7] The Truth and Reconciliation Commission (TRC) described the SLP before the onset of the civil conflict, as "incompetent," "corrupt," an exploitative instrument to be used by the government to terrorize political opponents, and ever ready to violate basic human rights of the Sierra Leonean people.[8] Ironically, at the frontline of domestic security is the Sierra Leone Police. The Justice Sector Reform clearly defined the role of the Sierra Leone Police—to serve and protect the Sierra Leonean people within the rule of law. Since the police organization is critical to the sustainable implementation of the criminal justice system, several training programs are organized to ensure professionalism within the police force so it is able to carry on its duties and responsibilities efficiently and effectively.[9]

Donors such as the German Technical Team (GTZ) and the British government have been very instrumental in helping the Sierra Leone government to equip its police force with the necessary training they need. The police service has undergone training, for instance, in the area of map reading to enable the service to identify specific locations during emergencies. GTZ has also assisted in the renovating of dilapidated police barracks. However, equipment and other logistics lag behind; this is a challenge to the effectiveness of the police service.

The Republic of Sierra Leone Armed Forces (RSLAF) has also received assistance from the International Military Assistance and Training Team (IMATT) which was created after the war to help transform the RSLAF into a self-sustaining, democratically sensitive force. Countries such as Britain, the United States, Ghana, Jamaica, Canada, Nigeria, have contributed more than one hundred high level military personnel to ensure the success of the program, and to enable the Sierra Leone government to secure its internal security as well as its territorial integrity. Like the police, the military is also poorly equipped. Weapons used are outdated and ineffective to conduct any meaningful and successful operations.

DECENTRALIZATION OF DOMESTIC SECURITY

Decentralizing domestic security in Sierra Leone is one of the fundamental security strategy put in place to seriously address security in the post-conflict. The reforms and networks are well integrated to achieve these objectives.

The National Security and Central Intelligence Act, 2002

The National Security and Central Intelligence Act, established by an act of Parliament in 2002 when the war was officially ended, was to be the main Sierra Leonean government document to ensure domestic security. The Act establishes a new security network in Sierra Leone which comprises the development of both internal and external security goals for the country. Under this Act, several other security agencies are to be established. This includes the National Security Council (NSC), the Central Intelligence and Security Unit (CISU), the Office of National Security (ONS), the Provincial Security Committee (PROSEC), and the District Security Committee (DISEC). The main objective is to coordinate domestic security and also to protect the territorial integrity of Sierra Leone.

National Security Council (NSC)

The National Security Council (NSC) is the forum that sets broad policy framework regarding Sierra Leone's internal and external security matters and strategy. As the commander-in-chief, the president is the chairman of the NSC.[10] Other members of the NSC include the Inspector General of Police (IGP), the Chief of Defense Staff, the Ministers of Foreign and Internal Affairs. The NSC's function is to coordinate the activities of security agencies and gather relevant information to formulate a broad framework to ensure security within Sierra Leonean communities.[11] As a forum for coordination, NSC establishes a better security organization in the country.

The Central Intelligence and Security Unit (CISU)

Under the authority of the president, CISU would collect all intelligence relating to threats to the internal and external security of the country.[12] This includes threats such as espionage, terrorism, and other internal activities that have the potential of destabilizing or overthrowing a duly elected government. External threats and attacks that have the potential of destabilizing the state is a major concern for the government. The onset and intensity of the civil conflict in Sierra Leone stemmed from the civil war in neighboring Liberia. Charles Taylor,[13] the then president of Liberia, was an active participant and played a significant role in the conflict in Sierra Leone.[14] Not only did he offer a safe haven for the Sierra Leonean rebels and their leader, Foday Sankoh, he also offered monetary resources and supplied the rebels with arms. The rebel attack threatened personal securities of the Sierra Leonean people residing near the eastern border (Kailahun district) with Liberia and later spread across the country when the rebel activities extended to the capital, Freetown.

Office of National Security (ONS)

The Office of National Security (ONS) is, by far, a hub for a comprehensive security network that the country has ever had. ONS is located in the Office of the President, but operates as an independent agency. During the eleven years of civil conflict, the government was unable to coordinate the security agencies throughout the country. Thus after the war, the objective was to re-establish a safe and secured environment for the people. Among the objectives of establishing the ONS was for the government of Sierra Leone to regain the confidence of the citizens and to provide the assurance that the government is capable of protecting its citizens and resources.

The British government, through the Department for International Development (DfID), finances the budget of the ONS. The British government provides training and other logistical support to ensure that there is continuity of skilled personnel at the ONS and also to enhance the agency's independence. Labor turnover in the public sector employment is very high in developing states with Sierra Leone not being an exception. Some of the consequences of this trend include acute corruption, low labor output, and inefficiencies in public sector administration. Sierra Leone, like other states in the developing world, electoral politics affect labor turnover in the public service. Patrimonialism and patronage are so well entrenched in the Sierra Leonean society.[15] The ONS, under the normal administrative circumstances, should have been a public service department in the office of the president, and its staff controlled by the president. However, the British government is fully aware of the chronic public service labor turnover after elections, and also the indispensable role of the ONS in assisting with post-conflict security in Sierra Leone. As a result, it is holding on to the "power of the purse"[16] as leverage to share in the control and management of the ONS with the Sierra Leonean government. ONS, therefore, operates as a semi-independent agency within the office of the president. Since its establishment in 2002, DfID has ensured that the existing ONS personnel continue to be at post even after elections whiles new employees are recruited and trained both in Sierra Leone and Britain when necessary. This has resulted in increased efficiency with which the ONS has performed its responsibilities, culminating in improved and effective domestic security outcomes.[17] The ONS has gained the confidence of the Sierra Leonean people who come to provide support whenever the Office of National Security is threatened with government influence in order to safeguard the independence of ONS. For instance, Sayoh Kamara[18] called on the president, Ernest Bai Koroma, not to heed to influential members of his own party to interfere with the operations and independence of the ONS. Sayoh Kamara described the calls by APC's high ranking officials to the president to remove the head of the ONS, Brigadier (rtd.) Kellie Hassan Conteh, as chairman of the national security coordinator was an attempt "to destroy one of Salone's success stories."[19]

Provincial Security Committee (PROSEC)

For administrative purposes, Sierra Leone is divided into three provinces and one area. The provinces are Northern, Eastern, and Southern Provinces. The area, also known as the Western Area, is made up of the capital, Freetown, and its surroundings. The Western Area is divided into two sections: the Western urban which comprises the state's capital, Freetown, and the Western rural constituting the surrounding areas of Freetown such as Waterloo, Benguema, York, Leicester, and Koya.

At the provincial level, PROSEC operates as an arm of the NSC as part of the security sector decentralization for better organization and effective control of security within Sierra Leone's provinces. The lack of information at the provincial level made it difficult for the government of Sierra Leone to strategize and to deploy security personnel to the various provinces to forestall the rebel advancement at the onset and during the civil war. PROSEC's responsibility is to execute all the functions allocated to it by the NSC; more importantly, it is to provide early warning signals and other security information to the NSC regarding potential threats to communities and government of Sierra Leone.[20] The Provincial Minister is the chair of PROSEC and some of its members include the Provincial Police Commander and a local military commander that is designated to the Committee. PROSEC meets every two weeks.

District Security Committee (DISEC)

Like the PROSEC, DISEC further coordinates the security situation at the district level. Sierra Leone is divided into twelve districts.[21] On the security decentralization chart, DISEC is at the lower level as compared with PROSEC, and is much closer to the people than PROSEC. DISEC's membership is representative of relevant actors and shows a more engaged community leaders and other individuals involved in planning and discussing security issues at the district level. Members of DISEC include the District Chief Executive who chairs the Committee, the district police commander, the chairman of the town council, the chairman of the Council of Chiefs, the local military commander, and the district security coordinator—who is the representative from the ONS. These are individuals who are opinion leaders in their respective communities and have a lot of respect, confidence, and trust from members of the community. Citizens can approach any member of DISEC and report any suspicious activities that threaten security within the communities.

DISEC's responsibility is to carry out any directives from the NSC, and to watch out for early warning signals regarding threat to security within the district that could destabilize the district and the entire country.[22] DISEC meets on a weekly basis. The District Chief Executive, who is also a member of the PROSEC gather the weekly security details and forwards it to PROSEC meetings that are held every two weeks. At the biweekly PROSEC meetings, all the districts in the provinces have the opportunity to come together to share security concerns in their neighborhoods which could impact the respective securities of their people both within the districts and the provinces.

Local Council

The local council has a role to play in the decentralization and coordination of security in the Sierra Leone. The local council is involved in the training of the police force. The goal is to develop a highly professionalized police force which would enforce the rule of law and also respect the rights of the Sierra Leonean people. The lack of an educated and professionalized police force was noted as one of the deficiencies of the Sierra Leone police,[23] and which affected their ability to protect the people during the war. Thus, the goal here is to ensure that not only do the police carry weapons in the towns or cities during patrols, but are also able to enforce the rule of law in the performance of their duties.

Substantial donor support, including 20 million pounds sterling from the UK government, helped in the training of the Sierra Leonean police in strategic and operational planning. Currently, Sierra Leoneans do commend the professionalism of the SLP, though there are a few isolated situations where the police was cited for human rights abuses or total negligence of duty. For instance there are cases where the police had not followed up with complaints of domestic violence, rape, assaults, and even murder.[24] The SLP, in defense, have argued the lack of logistics and equipment as hindering their ability to discharge their responsibilities effectively.

Other prevalent signals that show traces of fragile security and need to be addressed are the frequent organization of peace conferences and workshops that are held throughout the country. Since 2002, and almost ten years after the civil war was officially declared ended, peace workshops/conferences are a routine in Sierra Leone. Such workshops and conferences, though encouraged, are indications of the volatile nature of the security situation, and the depth of insecurity that people are living in. The peace workshops are as a result of sudden outbreaks of violence in the capital and other cities, and an evidence of the extent to which fear has had a grip on the society. Sierra Leoneans still have doubts about the state of security in the country. The consequences are that not only is human security affected but also the entire post-conflict recovery process is hampered; this has a negative effect on the country's development.

Community Based Organizations (CBOs)

Community Based Organizations (CBOs), though not part of the official security network in Sierra Leone, play a very important role in enhancing personal security within Sierra Leonean communities in the post-conflict. Women Action for Human Dignity (WAHD), located in the Northern Province capital of Makeni, runs a radio program to educate women on security issues and also provides information on resources that are available, should women personal securities be threatened.[25] Domestic violence issues are top on the agenda of issues discussed. The local police and prominent women are invited to be on the panel to discuss the security situation within communities. There is also time for phone-in sessions when people can call in to the radio station and share their personal security experiences and suggest ways to improve security. Eventually, there were suggestions that the program should involve the men in the community since men are the perpetrators of the crimes against women such as domestic violence, rape, and murder. The male involvement brought a new twist to the radio program and made it more comprehensive and engaging.

Youth organizations throughout the country have also been actively involved in enhancing security in the country. The objective has been to mobilize the youth to eschew violence and to involve themselves in the nation's transition to peace consolidation and development. The Kenema Youth Alliance (KYA) in the Eastern Province, for instance, partners with both local and international NGOs to organize security workshops for the youth in Kenema and its surroundings.[26] Since the youth were mostly those that were recruited to fight the war, it is imperative that they also be involved in the development of the communities they once destroyed and for which they currently live. By confronting the youth with these realities, they are challenged to commit to the development of their community and the country as a whole. The Kenema Youth Alliance, like other youth organizations throughout the country, has also been able to organize programs to integrate the youth into the mainstream development process. Consequently, the youth have served as election monitors, civil society advocates on human rights issues, and also involved themselves in youth campaigns.

Local and International NGOs

Both local and international NGOs have had roles to play in strengthening security within Sierra Leone. The Center for Democracy and Human Rights (CDHR), an NGO located in Kenema, promotes human rights culture and participatory governance at the grassroots level. This is achieved through information dissemination, advocacy, lobbying, dialogue forum, and civil education. It also organizes meetings and workshops for local chiefs, women, and the youth regarding human rights issues and the need to respect human rights. CDHR also participates in the district security meetings and share people's experiences on related security issues.[27]

The Global Rescue Mission (GRM), an international NGO, works in partnership with the police in sensitizing street boys who sometimes pose security risk to the society. In partnership with the Sierra Leone Action Network on Small Arms (SLANSA),[28] human security forums are organized with regard to the role of the community in sustainable security. It also holds consultative meetings with politicians, traditional rulers, and other stakeholders on the issue of security within Sierra Leone. GRM also partners with community-based organizations and local NGOs to organize security-sensitized workshops for communities in both urban and rural areas.[29]

Role of Traditional Chiefs

A traditional chief's status, in principle, makes the incumbent the custodian of moral values within the society which include issues of security and development. In the post-conflict, such moral influence is vital in terms of the chieftaincy institution's role in helping to ensure security in the community. Chiefs establish by-laws for a safe community. Most importantly, these by-laws also stipulate behavior conducts expected of new entrants in the community. Any stranger that relocates to another village needs to inform the chief about their presence and what they intend to do in the community.[30] It is in the best interest of strangers to follow this procedure. Firstly, it enables people in the community to know exactly what a stranger's intensions are so they do not look suspicious. Secondly, it enables the leadership of the village to extend the needed help should a stranger become involved in a dispute. A stranger's relatives could also be contacted in case of emergency.

Chiefs also serve as the frontline entities that receive reports of suspicious activities that threaten security within the community. It is also the responsibility of members of the community to report potential activities that could jeopardize the security of the community. Chiefs are often available to hear what the concerns of the community are regarding potential threats. Such threats are taken seriously by the chiefs. Being the custodians of morals and also the managers of the community's resources, an unsecured community becomes extremely costly for the chiefs. During the eleven-year civil war, most of the chiefs took refuge in big cities such as Freetown. As a result, they lost the source of their income, and their homes were destroyed. In addition to that, their dignity, respect, and recognition in the places they took refuge were reduced.[31] As most of them struggle to rebuild their communities at the end of the war, the goal and expectation is that such destabilizing phenomenon does not occur anymore in the future. It is therefore in their self-interest to ensure that their community's security is an utmost priority. Chiefs' membership in the DISEC is critical since they have numerous sources of information regarding security from their respective communities.[32]

United Nations Development Program (UNDP)

The United Nations Development Program (UNDP) has also played a significant role in Sierra Leone's post-conflict security environment. Small arms continue to be a threat to the security of the Sierra Leonean people and communities. UNDP organizes a series of forums and workshops to help address these security issues. One such initiative is the Arms for Development programs. The program was launched in 2007 as a joint initiative of the UNDP and the Sierra Leonean government.[33] The main goal of the Arms for Development program is to create sustainable peace, enhance human security, and achieve socioeconomic development. Among the objectives to be achieved include the voluntary surrender and collection of small arms in the community in exchange for development projects, national capacity building, and to ensure that Sierra Leone's borders are secured.

Though the arms for development project is deemed successful, targeted objectives are still at a snail's pace. UNDP has noted that the difficulty in enacting fire arms legislation in Sierra Leone is contributing to the slow pace of anticipated targets. Another factor contributing to this slow pace of envisaged developmental goals is the difficulty in building human capacity within Sierra Leone. The high rate of illiteracy is a burden on any attempt to build human capacity. The Sierra Leone government and donors have found it very difficult to overcome the high illiteracy rate and, thus, capacity building as a catalyst in stimulating development has not been realized. There are also traces of donor fatigue in helping to rebuild the country. The Arms for Development program only allocated $14,000 for such development projects.[34] This amount is woefully inadequate to sustain any meaningful developmental project. In mid-2007, the UNDP revised the community development start-up capital to $30,000.[35] However, this is still inadequate since most of the country's basic governing institutions are not in existence and need to be constructed instead of [re]constructed. Huge amounts of financial and other resources need to be committed to establish effective and efficient institutions in the post-conflict.

The problem in Sierra Leone is not the difficulty in collecting the small arms from the people, but the extent to which people's expectations are met in relation to how quickly sustainable development projects are implemented to keep idle hands busy. Since human beings are rational, the default is that they would want to have access to sophisticated arms if they believe that choice give them maximum benefits than the developmental projects the UNDP has created and continue to create.

NOTES

1. See David A. Lake and Donald Rothchild. 1996. "Containing Fear: The Origins and Management of Ethnic Conflict." *International Security*, Vol. 21, No. 2 (autumn), p. 41
2. These are freedom of speech, freedom of worship, freedom from want, and freedom from fear.
3. This was between May 2000 and May 2001
4. This included Executive Outcomes, the South African based private military organization
5. *Sobels* was the term coined for the portions of the Sierra Leone Army (SLA) that switched their allegiance back and forth between the government and the RUF. See *New York Times* article "Sierra Leone Rebels halted near capital but active elsewhere" by Norimitsu Onishi. May 12, 2000. http://www.nytimes.com/2000/05/12/world/sierra-leone-rebels-halted-near-capital-but-active-elsewhere.html?pagewanted=1.

6. See Sarah Meek. 2003. "Policing Sierra Leone." In Malan, M., Meek, S., Thusi, T., Ginifer, J., and Coker, P. (eds.) *Sierra Leone: Building the Road to Recovery*. Monograph 80. Pretoria: Institute for Security Studies. p. 1

7. See K. Biddle. 2000. "Conflict, Security, and Development," *Group Bulletin*, March-April: p. 1

8. See Sierra Leone Truth and Reconciliation Commission, Provisional Report, 2004, 3a: 77

9. See Bruce Baker. 2005. "Who do People Turn to for Policing in Sierra Leone?" *Journal of Contemporary African Studies*, Vol. 23 (3), (September) p. 376.

10. See Government of Sierra Leone: The National Security and Central Intelligence Act. Enacted by the President and Members of Parliament in July 2002. *A supplement to the Sierra Leone Gazette Extraordinary, Vol. CXXXIV, No. 42.* p. 3

11. Ibid., p. 4.

12. Ibid., p. 10.

13. The International Court of Justice (ICJ) in The Hague indicted Charles Taylor for crimes against humanity during the Sierra Leone civil war. He is now a convicted war criminal and sentenced to fifty years in jail after a very long trial session.

14. See Yekutiel Gershoni. 1997. "War without End and an End to War: The Prolonged Wars in Liberia and Sierra Leone." *African Studies Review*, Vol. 40, No. 3 (December), p. 55

15. See Paul Richards. 1996. *Fighting for the Rain Forest: War, Youth and Resources in Sierra Leone.* London: Villiers Publications, p. 34. Also, Paul Richards. 2001. "Are 'Forest' Wars in Africa Resource Conflicts? A Case of Sierra Leone" In *Violent Environments*. Nancy Lee Peluso and Michael Watts (eds.) New York: Cornell University Press, p. 69

16. The British government's Department for International Development (DfID) finances the budget of the Office of National Security (ONS).

17. This information was obtained from my source at the ONS.

18. Sayoh Kamara's article titled "APC Detractors want to destroy one of Salone's success stories" appeared in the *Awareness Times* newspaper, Freetown, October 15, 2009.

19. See Sayoh Kamara, "APC Detractors want to destroy one of Salone's Success Stories." Article appearing in the *Awareness Times* newspaper, Freetown. October 15, 2009.

20. See Government of Sierra Leone: The National Security and Central Intelligence Act. Enacted by the President and Members of Parliament in July 2002. *A supplement to the Sierra Leone Gazette Extraordinary, Vol. CXXXIV, No. 42.* p. 6

21. The Northern Province is made up of five districts, namely: Port Lokko, Kambia, Bombali, Koinadugu, and Tonkolili; the Eastern province is made up of 3 districts, namely: Kono, Kenema, Kailahun; the Southern province is made up of 4 districts, namely: Bonthe, Bo, Pujehun, and Moyamba.

22. See Government of Sierra Leone: The National Security and Central Intelligence Act. Enacted by the President and Members of Parliament in July 2002. *A supplement to the Sierra Leone Gazette Extraordinary, Vol. CXXXIV, No. 42.* p. 7

23. See Bruce Baker. 2005. "Who do People turn to for Policing in Sierra Leone?" *Journal of Contemporary African Studies*, Vol. 23 (3), (September) p. 376.

24. This is from an interview I had with the head of Women's Action for Human Dignity (WAHD) at Makeni, the capital of the Northern Province.

25. Information obtained from the interview I had with the leader of WAHD in Makeni in the Northern Province.

26. Information obtained through the interview of the leader of the Kenema Youth Alliance in Kenema, capital of the Eastern province.

27. Information regarding the operations of CDHR was obtained through interviews with its officials at Makeni.

28. SLANSA was created in 2001 as part of an effort to ensure sustainable security in Sierra Leone. It is network of religious as well as civil society organizations that advocate for control of small arms and light weapons. It is part of the International Action Network on Small Arms (IANSA).

29. Information regarding the operations of GRM was obtained through interviews with its officials at Kenema.

30. This information was obtained in an interview with the Paramount Chief in Makeni.

31. See Bruce Baker. 2005. "Who do People Turn to for Policing in Sierra Leone?" *Journal of Contemporary African Studies*, Vol. 23 (3), (September), p. 381

32. See Government of Sierra Leone: The National Security and Central Intelligence Act. Enacted by the President and Members of Parliament in July 2002. *A supplement to the Sierra Leone Gazette Extraordinary, Vol. CXXXIV, No. 42*, p. 6

33. See UNDP Sierra Leone. Arms for Development. End of Year Progress report. 2007, p. 2

34. Ibid., p. 3.

35. Ibid., p. 6

Chapter Six

Human Security and Sierra Leone's Post-Conflict Reforms

The preceding chapters dealt with the underlying causes of the conflict in Sierra Leone. They argue that the fundamental cause of the conflict in Sierra Leone was the fact that human security had been largely ignored. This book has also provided information on the post-conflict reforms the government has put in place to address this issue. This section of the book examines these reforms and their effect on human security.

HUMAN SECURITY AND THE SECURITY DISCOURSE

Embedded in the concept of human security is the fact that a state cannot be a passive actor but rather charged with the responsibility of creating an enabling domestic environment conducive for human security. However, the relevance of human security to the security discourse goes far beyond a particular state. Not only does it have implications on domestic security and stability, but also impacts on regional and international security. At the regional level, the failure of individual states to address issues of human security has led to the increase in the number of internally displaced persons (IDPs) within the state and refugees in neighboring states. Xenophobic attitudes are also widespread in Africa where migrants are subjected to various forms of harassments and, in some cases, deaths. For instance, Zimbabweans who fled the March 2008 post-election crisis suffered the wrath of angry South Africans who, fearing they may lose their jobs as a result of the mass influx, harassed and even killed some of the fleeing Zimbabweans. In Europe, xenophobic attitudes have led to attacks on migrants from neighboring states. In North America, especially the United States, it has led to aspects of racial profiling. The critical aspect of human security and its implication on state security is that the consequences of deteriorating human security situation that leads to movements of people from one state to another also exposes latent human security problems in other states, including the developed ones. State institutions shape the domestic behaviors over time. In the same manner, critical institutions that enhance human security need to be consciously developed over time.

At the international level, states are concerned that the deterioration in human security conditions is a threat to global security. Failed and weak states which have non-existent or weak institutions and lack other state structures to safeguard human security have become havens for global security threat. States such as Somalia, Yemen, and Afghanistan pose a security challenge to themselves and their respective sub-regions, and have now become havens for actors that threaten global security. Other states such as the DR Congo have become very volatile and present a dilemma with regard to how they will evolve and the respective challenges they may pose to the international community. There are mixed perceptions about the domestic revolution that took place in the Arab world.[1] Though the revolution, protests, and demonstrations are seen as good for a new wave of democracy in the mostly authoritarian Arab world, the global community is also concerned about the challenges it poses to global security. States such as the United States of America are skeptical and sometimes slow to support such protest due to fear that they may actually be supporting Islamists and extremists who may eventually pose a threat to international security. Again, Islamist occupation in certain parts of Africa has become a global security concern.

As interstate wars have waned, and intrastate conflicts threaten domestic and international security, human security becomes the go-to tool for resolving conflict and maintaining a sustainable post-conflict peace environment. As discussed earlier, conflicts stems from people's perception about a status quo, and their willingness to change that status quo. States, both de jure and de facto, establish state institutions to protect their sovereignty and territorial integrity. Financial, military, and other commitments are focused on achieving the goal of protecting state sovereignty. However, as the global security discourse shifted from state security to human security in the 1990s, states especially in the developing world have not committed enough resources to achieve human security. State leaders, even those in the developed world, have paid only lip service to human security. In some cases, we have seen traces of "security fatigue."[2] Security fatigue occurs not because of the lack of resources, but the sheer reluctance to commit such resources, since such actions do not have short-term political benefits. However, when the failure to commit resources at the front end metastases to full-blown international security crisis, resources are committed fully since the political benefits to states, especially in the advanced democratic world, are high. In the developing world where domestic security is fragile, the situation is more precarious. States' wealth, power, and influence depend on the worth of its human resources and human capacity building.

HUMAN SECURITY AND SIERRA LEONE'S POST-CONFLICT REFORMS

Why have states been less motivated to pursue actions that strengthen human security? This chapter discusses the human security framework from the underlying causes of the conflict in Sierra Leone. It also examines how the post-conflict reforms in the political, civil, economic, and personal securities arenas enhance stability and peace in post-conflict Sierra Leone. Human security involves humans; it captures the extent to which government policies impact positively on the lives of the people. In Sierra Leone, the relevance of human security could not have come at a more important time when one examines the causes of the conflict in the country. The information and other data used in this chapter are obtained through interviews conducted in the Eastern and Northern Provinces and Freetown and its surrounding areas. About one hundred interviews were obtained. Interviews were also done with government agencies, Members of Parliament (MPs), community-based organizations, media houses, and both local and international non-governmental organizations. The interviews highlight the fundamental and structural problems (breakdown of human security) that underlie the onset of the conflict. It also underscores the thesis of this book—human security needs to be the underlying factor in all conflict negotiations and post-conflict reforms. The Sierra Leonean conflict had its basis on structural weaknesses in all aspects of the Sierra Leonean society, including the politics, civil rights, economics, and the security of the people of which the human security paradigm seeks to address.

The interviews were divided into five sections. The first section was to ascertain the fundamental cause of the conflict from the perspective of the Sierra Leonean people. The objective of the second section of the interview questions was to find out the extent to which the political decentralization have been implemented, and also whether or not the Sierra Leonean people have the feeling that they are a significant part of the political process and government. It is one thing laying out a clear strategy to move Sierra Leone from war to sustainable peace; it is, however, another challenge for the objectives to be realized. The third section of the interview deals with issues of civil rights and how post-conflict Sierra Leone has been able to reassure its citizens that rule of law would be applied equitably irrespective of status and ethnic backgrounds. Notable among these is the confidence that the reform in the court system will re-establish the courts as the appropriate channels to settle disputes. Other important concerns such as how the government plans to ensure civil rights and liberties are also addressed. The objective of the fourth section of the interview was to obtain from the Sierra Leonean people the extent to which personal safety has improved since the declaration of end of war in 2002. This is very critical since community and state-wide safety is necessary for any government efforts at recovery and development. Cultivating and nurturing the culture of savings and investment of any kind depends, to a very large extent, on whether or not there is a guarantee of investment security, and invariably the assurance that returns and other benefits are realizable in the foreseeable future. When people perceive the environment to be secured, the better it is for them to engage proactively and pragmatically in developmental decisions and projects. Finally, the fifth section of the interview deals with the issues of employment opportunities in both the public and private sector.[3] What the book described as cash flow security is very relevant to any sustainable peace consolidation. It is not enough to use official unemployment data to make conflict predictions. Equally important is the potential of the informal sector and the ease with which opportunities exist for people to earn income to enhance their cash flow.

UNDERLYING CAUSE OF CONFLICT IN SIERRA LEONE: HUMAN SECURITY ISSUES

Sierra Leoneans have a plethora of reasons for the onset of the civil war in 1991. Among these reasons were the marginalization and exclusion of a significant portion of the Sierra Leonean population from participating in the political process, prevention of people from sharing in the benefits of the state's economic resources, bad governance on the part of political elites, endemic corruption, ethnic tensions, high unemployment and poverty rates, greed, low literacy rate, and social injustice. In the literature of civil conflict, ethnic tension and polarization become an overwhelming explanatory phenomenon of why civil wars occur. However, underlying the ethnic tension explanation is the role of institutions to either alleviate or escalate these tensions. For the most part, the reasons for the conflict onset highlight the extent to which non-existent or weak institutions could have a negative impact on the political functioning and stability of states, its development, and growth. It also demonstrates that strong and effective states do not just emerge. Effective institutions need to be consciously developed, continually committed to, and steered along a target goal.

About 21 percent (see figure 6.1) of Sierra Leoneans consider the culture of corruption as the major reason why the conflict occurred. In Sierra Leone, and most parts of Africa, the dynamics of corruption go beyond public offi-

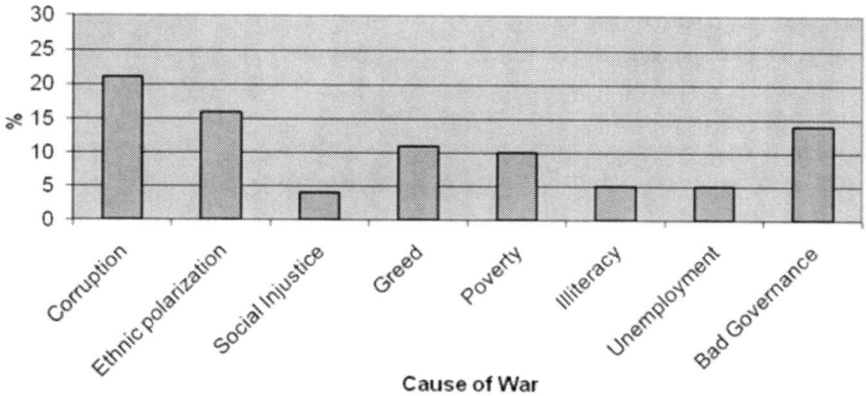

Figure 6.1. A graph showing Sierra Leoneans' perception of the onset of the civil conflict

cials using the privileged and entrusted positions in public office to secure favors or contracts now or in the future; it also involves the plundering and siphoning of limited state assets for personal wealth. Public officials turned to millionaires overnight, and live very luxurious lifestyles while the rest of the people who entrusted these positions to them watch with dismay as their personal economic securities deteriorate.

At its peak, corruption becomes endemic and its fangs overwhelm people who previously possess very high integrity. Corruption is a disincentive to development; it weakens one's ability to hold firm principles, and leads to a gloomy future prospect for the population at large. As the window of opportunity for addressing the negative impact of corruption seemed shut, the people are left with no other alternative than to change the status quo, by picking up arms and overthrowing those in authority. In Sierra Leone, the government has taken the issue of corruption seriously and has hoisted giant billboards across the nation's capital and throughout big cities and small towns across the country. Many Sierra Leoneans believe that the establishment of the Anti-Corruption Commission (ACC) is a positive step for addressing the corruption pandemic. In the literature of the causes of civil conflict, this finding becomes significant since it shifts the debate from primordial causes of civil wars to a structural and institutional forum for analyzing the cause of conflict. In spite of the benefits of the Anti-Corruption Commission, it has had its own challenges since its establishment in 2000. Some of the challenges include the unwillingness on the part of the Commission to execute its mandate. It is not surprising that in November 2005 the head of the Commission, Valentine Collier was sacked when he was accused of being involved in corruption. In October of 2007, Henry Joko-Smart, who was then the chair of the Commission was also removed from his post after being accused of his reluctance to move corruption prosecutions forward. Since 2008, the Commission has aggressively pursued corruption charges and convictions of former and current public officeholders. The sentences however, have not been punitive enough to deter acts of corruption. Those convicted have the option to pay hefty fines or serve prison terms. Since these individuals are well connected with the political and economic elites, or have already amassed enough wealth for themselves, the payment of the fine is usually their preference to jail times. Many critics of the Commission have accused it of being a "phony" institution meant to appease donors and other investors who are desperate to see corruption eradicated from Sierra Leone before they commit to any assistance for the country.

Corruption is a recurring phenomenon in Sierra Leone, so is the state's inability to deal with the problem. However, the situation provides an excellent opportunity to reexamine the phenomenon and the framework within which it recurs in Sierra Leone and other African societies. A re-analysis of the corruption phenomenon has implications regarding the institutions and strategies needed to deal with the corruption epidemic. Currently, the Anti-Corruption Commission has three major goals: prevent, educate, and prosecute corruption. Dealing with the issue of corruption is a challenge in certain societies. I do not intend to argue that some cultures, by default, are corruption prone. However, certain cultural practices are susceptible to acts of corruption, especially, when family and community status is at stake and highly cherished or guarded. The extended family system and the demands it places on some few members of the family overwhelms those individuals which make them succumb to acts of corruption. Embedded in most cultures in sub-Saharan Africa is the respect and the great responsibility placed on the "older one" and people in public positions. For instance, if an uncle visits a niece or nephew, the younger one (niece or nephew) expects or demands a present or gift from the older one (uncle). In most cases, the uncle feels compelled to supply the gift as an honor and also to protect his status. When the exchange of gift does not happen during contact, disappointment and bad feelings is the outcome at both ends. This same relationship is also prevalent at the highest level of politics and the society. Some people in a constituency literally demand that their representatives[4] offer cash or in-kind gift when a contact is made. Representatives also feel the urgency to supply such presents as a sign of respect of their status in society. The economic model of price determination on the market concludes that the equilibrium price is the price at which the market is cleared since quantities demanded equates quantity supplied at that price. However, the interplay of demand and supply in terms of the expectations on society leaders does not result in such equilibrium. The demand from constituents overwhelms the personal abilities and resources of representatives to meet such demands and maintain the respect and status. To make up for the shortage, those in positions of public trust turn toward acts of corruption. Though this is not an excuse for betraying public trust, it brings into the debate the socio-cultural discourses and its impact on strategies to reduce or eliminate corruption. In Sierra Leone, some complain that their Members of Parliament do not visit the constituency frequently. In fact, what this may mean is that when the Member of Parliament visited, there was not such exchange of cash or in-kind gifts.

Corruption, no matter the intensity, results in inefficiencies in societies. Though the number of arrests and convictions of people involved in acts of corruption has increased, there are no signs that such behaviors will be halted in the foreseeable future. Thus, serious attention should be directed toward socio-cultural factors in addressing the issue of corruption. From a human security perspective, corruption is more than using public office to gain influence and wealth. It undercuts the effort at building human capacities, especially in post-conflict states. This is so because only few people have the privilege to hold public office, and when they do, they concentrate or distribute resources among their close-knit networks. This leaves out the majority of the people who, ironically, need to be empowered for a stronger and sustainable post-conflict era.

Also, some Sierra Leoneans perceive the tension between the ethnic groups (Temne and Mende) is one of the leading causes of the conflict. This perception is in line with the Primordialist argument in the literature of the Sierra Leonean civil conflict which states that the inherent in-group/out-group consciousness triggers societal instability.[5] Ethnic tensions in Sierra Leone include rivalries and sheer animosity between the ethnic groups. Figure 6.1 shows that 16 percent of Sierra Leoneans believe that ethnic tension is a challenge the government needs to address in the post-conflict. This is a critical issue since the perception of ethnic tension was consistent among those in the southeastern part of the country and those from the north. Ethnic tension polarizes the state and affects state institutions without being noticed. Northern Sierra Leoneans align with political parties and elites who are northerners by virtue of the fact that they speak the Temne language, or bear a northern name such as Koroma, Kamara, among others. People in the Eastern and Southern provinces, predominantly Mende areas, also align themselves with political parties and elites emanating from those provinces. The Western Area, comprising of Freetown and its surrounding areas become a battle ground for the struggle for power between the Temne and the Mende ethnic groups.

Ethnic tension is a personal security issue, which is a critical part of human security. Political elites benefit from the tension because it largely determines who secures political power to govern. The fear of the other becomes a rallying point during the general and other elections, consequently fueling those tensions. Though Sierra Leone elites seem to refrain from explicitly supporting ethnic tensions, their actions show their implicit support, invariably institutionalizing the already deteriorating personal security situation. In the post-conflict, it is important for governments to explicitly develop and implement strategies toward reducing or eliminating ethnic tensions. When it comes to addressing a situation where ethnic favoritism is present, mere words are not enough; what is needed is actions. Appointing cabinet ministers from the different ethnic groups and awarding government contracts to people from different backgrounds will be a good starting point. The challenge of co-opting people from the opposing political aisle is usually not well received by supporters of the incumbent party. Besides, it is a daunting initiative in the short term. However, the long-term benefit ensures a stable society free of tension. Elites have to understand that security for their own people ensures their own political viability and leadership security.

In Figure 6.1, 14 percent of Sierra Leoneans consider marginalization, exclusion, and bad governance as significant causes of the conflict. This finding comes as no surprise, especially when corruption is considered the top trigger of the conflict. When corruption becomes endemic and only a few political elites control the most of the state's resources, there are very few resources left for the majority of the people. In order for elites to hold on to power and also to improve their public image, a few groups of people[6] are selected to participate in the limited resources.[7] The consequence is the marginalization and exclusion of some ethnic groups from the equitable distribution of the nation's resources. Bad governance[8] is a consequent of marginalization and exclusion. Not only is a majority of the people excluded from the governing process, but government also become less concerned about improving the human capacity of these people. When bad governance is entrenched within the society, government refuses to establish appropriate institutions where individuals could channel their grievances through the political process. Other causes of the conflict include greed, poverty, unemployment, illiteracy, and social injustice as shown in figure 6.1. In the post-conflict, good governance with a commitment to involve citizens in the governing process is essential to a stable society and development.

The perception of Sierra Leoneans of the causes of the conflict reflects fundamental institutional and structural deficiencies that have plagued the country since independence. Sierra Leone's political elites are more prone to creating dysfunctional structures to enable them to oppress other ethnicities and to empower others.[9] These are fundamental problems which could be resolved through human security approaches when elites could see the benefit of such an approach and the political will to do so. The reforms embarked upon by the Sierra Leonean government with the help of donors and other international stakeholders address some of the root causes of the conflict. This involve re-implementing, and substantially restructuring and revitalizing existing weak institutions such as the Local Government Act that was suspended in 1972 and the creation of new institutions such as the Anti-Corruption Commission (ACC) and the office of the ombudsman.

The Sierra Leonean people were war weary and have lost any hope of a positive future for the country as a result of the prolonged war. The Lome and Abidjan Peace Accords and the declaration of the end of war in 2002 brought a much-needed respite. About 43 percent of Sierra Leoneans noted that the declaration of the end of war signified freedom, and about 37 percent said it signified peace (see figure 6.2). To most people, therefore, the declaration of the end of conflict in 2002 has brought freedom of movement to engage in normal daily activities that enhance their lives and restore the confidence of productive living. It also signifies a new dawn of peace and hope for the country's future. The conflict experience, it is believed, is an opportunity to analyze the dynamism of war and peace and to appreciate peaceful societal environment and the need to ensure sustainable peace at all levels. About 10 percent, 6 percent, and 4 percent (see figure 6.2) of Sierra Leoneans believe that the declaration of the end of war signifies development, assurance of government control and protection, and stability, respectively. This has implications for the human security/development nexus as we examine the proverbial "chicken and egg" scenario regarding whether or not development leads to the achievement of human security or vice versa. Overall, 20 percent of Sierra Leoneans believe that the end of the war will bring about development and stability. When this number is compared to the eighty percent who see the end of war as fundamentally critical for freedom and peace, it is clear that while development and growth have a trickle-down effect that could be a necessary condition for creating an environment of human security, they are not sufficient conditions for guaranteeing human security. Achieving human security poses serious challenges for some states in advanced economies. Economic turmoil in Europe has implications on

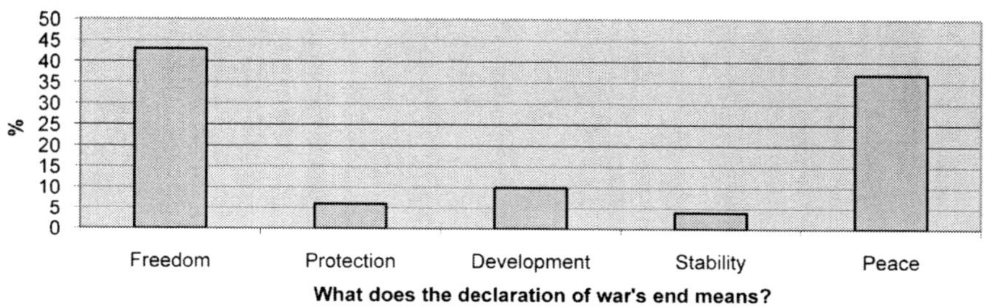

Figure 6.2. A graph showing the general feelings among the Sierra Leonean people when the war was declared ended

human security. The Sierra Leonean people want peace and freedom to be established first. Development and growth are therefore offshoots of an environment of established human security. As argued at the beginning of the book, human security is an independent variable which drives development, stability, and growth within states.

More than half (see figure 6.3) of Sierra Leoneans believe that some of the causes of the conflict were resolved when the war was declared ended in 2002 and that there were signs that the government had taken steps to address the root causes of the conflict. This perception has implications regarding the extent to which the Sierra Leonean people will be receptive to government actions and policies in the post-conflict era. Though 6 percent of Sierra Leoneans believe that the declaration of end of conflict meant that the government now has control over state institutions to ensure stability within Sierra Leonean societies, they also put a very high premium on the ability of government to lead the state. The confidence of the Sierra Leonean people in the government's ability to demonstrate leadership in the post-conflict is a critical indicator for sustainable post-conflict reforms. It is a measure of the people's readiness to work with the leadership in the post-conflict. At the time the war was declared ended in January 2002 major fighting between the government and the rebels had reduced, with only intermittent disturbances occurring at certain parts of the country. The respondents noted that the implementation of the 1996 Abidjan and the 1999 Lome Peace Accords contributed to the relatively calm situation. At the time, ex-combatants had been disarmed, demobilized, and reintegrated into the society. Most of the ex-combatants have also been given training in various skills and start-up kits to enable them start their own small businesses and stay out of trouble. When the people become war weary and can see some effort at attaining peace, they are more likely to appreciate the peaceful environment. In all 45 percent of Sierra Leoneans believe that the causes of war are still not fully

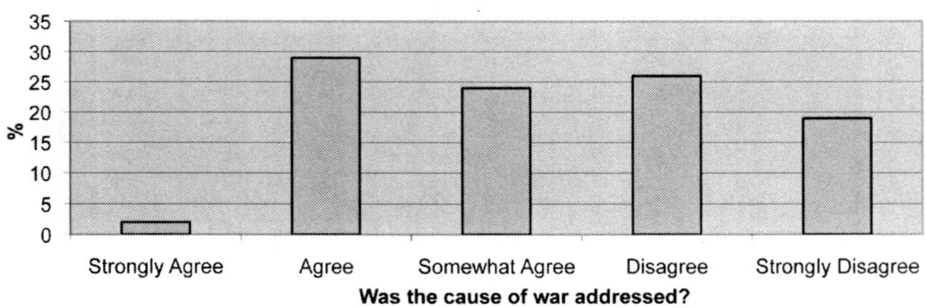

Figure 6.3. Graph showing whether the causes of war had been addressed when the war was declared ended

resolved. Also, corruption, marginalization, and bad governance are still in existence. Public officials still ride in luxurious state government vehicles, and the unemployment rate especially among the youth population is still on the rise.

Sierra Leoneans are very much aware about government actions and policy strategies to ensure sustainable post-conflict environment. Among these positive reforms include the Truth and Reconciliation Commission, Anti-Corruption Commission, the political decentralization process, and the skills training going on throughout the country. About 16 percent (see figure 6.4) of Sierra Leoneans believe that the Truth and Reconciliation Commission was a step in the right direction. The Commission provided an opportunity to confront the past. It also helped provide answers to very difficult questions regarding why Sierra Leoneans chose the path of destroying each other in order to appreciate the importance of cooperation in dealing with potential conflict situations should such situations occur in the future. Though the Truth and Reconciliation Commission's mandate ended in 2004 when its final report was finally completed, Sierra Leoneans believe it served the purpose of creating a forum that promoted discussion, healing, and reconciliation.

Figure 6.4 also shows 14 percent of Sierra Leoneans deem the establishment of the Anti-Corruption Commission necessary for a stable Sierra Leone since the Commission could address some institutional weaknesses and also establish the culture of accountability in public service. As human security is an all-encompassing phenomenon, and the government not only is the major employer in the developing world but also the one that initiates economic policy as well as the distributor of resources, economic and other cash-flow security are dependent on greater accountability on the part of public officials. As noted earlier, Sierra Leoneans blamed endemic corruption for the onset of the conflict; they also have confidence in the work of the ACC to

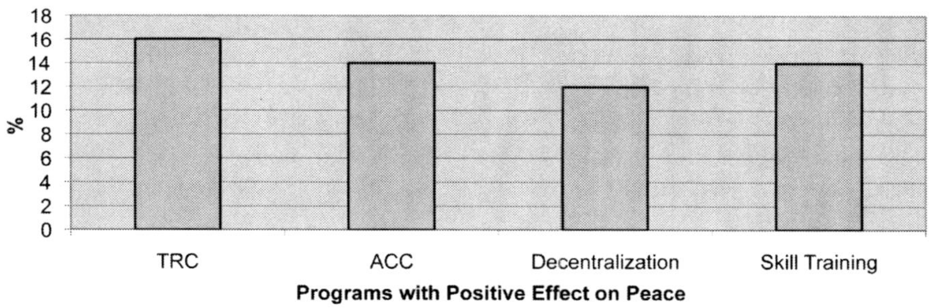

Figure 6.4. A graph showing institution and processes for sustainable post-conflict era

rein in corrupt public servants. The government has mounted numerous giant billboards by roadsides across the country to educate the people about the ills of corruption and also the imperativeness of reporting acts of corruption to the appropriate authorities.

Again, about 14 percent of Sierra Leoneans commend the government's effort at providing skills training to the youth to address the youth unemployment problem. The challenge, however, is that though the skills training emphasizes the attainment of entrepreneurial skills, there are reports that most trainees do not utilize the acquired skill to be entrepreneurs and establish their own businesses. Some have even sold the start-up equipments given to them to establish their businesses. These challenges point to opportunities for government to evaluate the reforms, especially with regard to the economy which seems to be the weakest link in the effort at building a stable after-conflict era. Are these skills training mere jobs training or an opportunity for career paths? Other important factors may include the existence of markets for the skills training. In the post-conflict, governments do not have much room to implement programs that are not viable. On the other hand, the people have no patience as they desperately wait for pragmatic strategies that will positively impact their lives.

The political reforms that decentralized political power from Freetown to the provinces, through the districts and the chiefdoms, and even to the head man level, and which also established some form of good governance is greatly appreciated by the Sierra Leonean people. In all, about 12 percent of Sierra Leoneans see the decentralization process as a step in the right direction, since it provides the opportunity for people to participate at some level of government. The political reforms correct the over-centralization of government in the period before and during the conflict. The 12 percent is however low. It is a signal that government has to do more to change this perception. Other positive governmental policies that were deemed positive to the consolidation of the peace in the country included the establishment of the special courts, the national youth policy, the Human Rights Commission, the DDR[10] program, and the educational policy which provides free basic education, and also expands polytechnic education across the country.

However, Sierra Leoneans believe that there are still some potential triggers that could plunge the country back to war if not seriously addressed. About 95 percent of Sierra Leoneans (see figure 6.5) believe that the probability exist for the country to retrogress and fall back into conflict. They cite the high unemployment and poverty rates, and the high political intolerance and tensions between political parties, as critical issues that could affect the fragile peace the country has enjoyed since 2002. The tension between the two leading political parties, the All People's Congress and the Sierra Leone People's Party, is evident across the country and during the 2012 election campaign. There have been instances where supporters, mostly the youth of

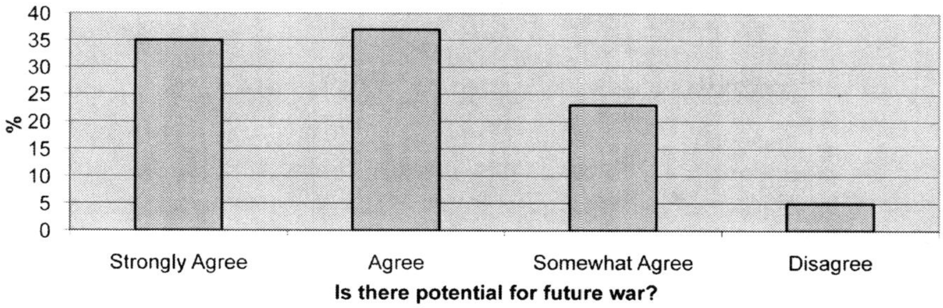

Figure 6.5. Graph showing the potential for future domestic conflict

one political party go on a rampage and destroy the party headquarters and assets of their opponents. Since 2002, peace workshops have become a regular phenomenon within Sierra Leonean societies. The Sierra Leonean government and international donors have constantly organized these peace workshops as a means to remind the youth about the consequences of the lack of respect and intolerance for others. Youth unemployment has become the Achilles' heel of post-conflict reforms in the country. Many refer to the high level of youth unemployment as a "ticking time bomb" situation, which will eventually explode.

The important piece of the political process that has dogged states transitioning to democracies is the electoral process. Embedded in democracy is transparency and equal opportunities in the political process resulting from pre-determined rules. However, the electoral process presents a dilemma to many states in Africa that are either willing or reluctant to embrace it. The paradox of elections is that the losing party, more often than not, vilifies it as unfair and even illegitimate, while the winning party hails the process. However, alternatives to elections are still yet to be found. Generally, the Sierra Leonean people have a positive attitude toward the electoral process and they deem the process as a good mechanism to forestall future conflict. The opportunity to hire and fire representatives to any level of government is seen as a latent power held by the people and used when needed. It also creates a sense of participation in the governmental process. The 2007 general elections that ushered in the All People's Congress party into government, is an indication of such confidence, and a demonstration that the electoral process actually works. Most Sierra Leoneans believe in the effectiveness of the electoral process as a good mechanism to prevent future conflict. While there is significant favorability toward the electoral process, Sierra Leoneans raise concerns that the process is only beneficial to the extent that they are able to elect their representatives. However, expected developmental programs are either slow to be implemented within the communities or such projects do not occur at all after they have been promised.

REFORMS AND POLITICAL PARTICIPATION

The political reform in Sierra Leone intends to decentralize the political space. Key objectives include political participation[11] and awareness, political engagement, and political accountability. These objectives have human security implications. Sierra Leone experienced only few years of post-independent democracy in the 1960s after which the country was plagued by authoritarian and military rule for the next three decades. Important elements of the political reform process in Sierra Leone include the electorates' newly acquired political power; votes do really count, in principle, and that they can elect their preferred candidates to represent them in government when duty calls on them to appear at the ballot box. Secondly, there are responsibilities associated with the political power. This responsibility includes making themselves accountable by being well informed of the choices that candidates offer and making officeholders accountable by letting them suffer electoral loses when representatives fall short of their responsibilities. Full participation of the people in government is one of the major provisions in the two peace accords. As has been noted in previous chapters, the Sierra Leonean government has been very active, at least in principle, to implement the provisions in the Local Government Act of 2004, and to involve the citizens in governance.

Participation and Consolidation

Participation in any form of a political process[12] has positive consequences for societies. Not only does it stabilize the existing system, it also consolidates the system because of the support it has from the people. The 2007 and 2012 general elections in Sierra Leone witnessed a very high turnout rate (estimated at 75.8 percent) which reflected the enthusiasm and the immense electoral power that the electorate has come to realize and its effect on government. Sierra Leoneans understood the opportunity that currently existed to determine the leadership of the state. The 2007 elections brought back the opposition party, All People's Congress (APC), after several years of political dominance by the Sierra Leone People's Party (SLPP). Most Sierra Leoneans see participation as a critical piece of the political stability puzzle, irrespective of the outcome of the elections. This is important since the Sierra Leonean people believed that the lack of participation in the political process is one of the major causes of the conflict. This perception needs to be nurtured by government by doubling down on institutions that strengthen the process. A great deal of excitement surrounded the 2012 general elections for two main contradictory reasons. First, sections of the Sierra Leonean population see the 2012 elections as another opportunity to elect preferred candidates. Others on the other hand see the elections as an opportunity to engage in activities of civil disturbances if their preferred candidates do not win. Sierra Leone political elites need to be aware that the peaceful environment that exists currently is fragile and this reality should incentivize the leadership to engage the people with regard to the development of society-specific institutions necessary for peace consolidation.

Sierra Leoneans are also appreciative of the ability to vote. They now have a voice and their vote also counts. The change in government brought about by the 2007 elections is evidence to that fact. They noted that enfranchisement make them feel part of the government. Others also noted the essential components of being part of the government which include the opportunity to present themselves as candidates for political positions, organizing forums to engage representatives regarding what their activities are in parliament and the city council, involvement in political education, and participating in local government. Unfortunately, they have not been able to actively engage their representatives at the local and district assemblies as well as parliament regarding development in their communities. Most are concerned about the continuous absenteeism of their representatives in the constituencies. This probably may be due to logistical hurdles such as the unavailability of vehicles, the lack of good roads, lack of access to processing and communication equipment, and the lack of appropriate and efficient staffing. These logistical issues could be addressed when seen as a priority. It is also worth mentioning that Sierra Leoneans acknowledge the challenges within which their representatives work.

Political Awareness

Much as the political process provides the opportunity to play a role in how governments form and function, Sierra Leoneans are aware of the issues that are fundamental to the political discourse and candidate choice. Though some scholars have highlighted the polarized nature of Sierra Leoneans societies, most people acknowledge that they had enough information about the respective candidates before they made their choices in the 2007 and 2012 elections. They also noted that they understood the political platforms that the candidates stood for. Notable among the candidates' platforms that electorates care about is the policy plans for sustainable development. Others were also concerned about a candidate's active participation in the development of the community, his/her integrity. Due to the strong regionalism that creates the tendency to vote for candidates from same ethnic backgrounds, it is very difficult to verify whether or not candidates' platforms guided voter choice. In that case, Freetown which is the most cosmopolitan breaks the deadlock and picks the winning party and government. Some also noted that they did not bother to listen to candidates' platforms because the candidates were imposed on their constituency. Winning elections in the post-conflict to form a government is not the most important issue when compared to the need to bring the people along the mechanism of government. From a human security point of view, bringing the people along is the fundamental aspect of the electoral process whether or not some constituencies complain that candidates were imposed on them. The act of voting is appreciated by most Sierra Leoneans. Since this is a critical measure of them being part of the political process, every effort should be made to encourage voting. Denying people the right to vote could lead to a situation where the electorates may develop apathy toward the electoral process. This is a serious human security threat, and can weaken the confidence the people have in elected officials.

Aside from the general election that receives greater attention in Sierra Leone, Sierra Leoneans also demonstrate a great deal of awareness of other elections. Local council, chieftaincy, and village head man elections are well participated. Since representatives at this lower-tier government are closer to the people, most Sierra Leoneans agree that the good relations they have with representatives at that level should be a model for their members of parliament (MPs). Thus they expect their MPs to be accessible to their constituents.

One significant element of political awareness which also has consequences on political tolerance is whether or not Sierra Leoneans vote along ethnic lines. Even though regionalism is deeply entrenched in Sierra Leonean societies, overall, only a third of Sierra Leoneans agree that ethnic background of a candidate influence their vote choice. Though it is difficult to clearly distinguish between regionalism, ethnicity, and candidate choice, in places such as cosmopolitan Freetown and its surroundings, this result is significant. About 89 percent in Freetown and 100 percent in Waterloo areas remarked that their choice decisions for candidates in the 2007 elections were not influenced by ethnicity. In the Northern Province, 75 percent of the respondents claimed ethnicity did not affect vote choice while only 20 percent of those in the Eastern and Southern Provinces noted that ethnicity did not affect their vote choice. Having full confidence and trust in leaders from the same ethnic group is one of the major characteristic of politics in many developing states including Sierra Leone. The implication is that people trust "the institution of our own kind" since that is the most effective institution that guarantees fairness. This is a human security issue in terms of the desire to accommodate people from different backgrounds into any meaningful and sustainable political reform. This is also the main reason why political leaders need to make the creation of effective institutions their main goal taking into consideration the diversity of their societies.

Political Accountability

Sierra Leoneans are of the opinion that elected representatives need to be held accountable for the positions that have been entrusted to their care. With corruption being one of the major causes of conflict, it is not surprising that the electorate demand accountability from public officials. Slightly more than half of the respondents acknowledge that, currently, public officials are not held accountable for their actions. They noted that elected officials do not deliver on campaign promises stipulated in their political platforms. About 48 percent of Sierra Leoneans believe elected officials should be accountable.

Another element of accountability has to do with how accessible elected officials are. Most Sierra Leoneans acknowledge they rarely have contact with their Members of Parliament (MPs). This is stunning. However, MPs on their part claim they make regular visits to their constituencies and have discussions with them. Reconciling these opposing claims regarding the extent of how accessible elected representative are is fundamental and has implications on government's role in ensuring integrity and trust in public office. One Member of Parliament offered an explanation. He believes the accessibility issue has more to do with the extent to which Members of Parliament are able to give some financial rewards when they visit their respective constituencies than their mere physical presence. The more an MP is able to visit their constituency, the higher the possibility that development projects will be embarked upon due to them being constantly reminded of their campaign promises. Developmental projects bring job opportunities and improved household incomes. In the absence of such projects, the alternative may well be the Members of Parliament providing the cash benefits (in-kind income) to augment disposable household incomes. Since the income of a Member of Parliament is not sufficient enough to embark on such large-scale perks in the constituency, the inclination to resort to acts of corruption is highest.

On the other hand, the lack of development projects at the constituency level impact negatively on any serious effort at political reforms in the country. MPs in the opposition complain that they are always discriminated against when it comes to the provision of funds to develop their constituencies. Thus, there are still unwritten structural impediments in governance that makes it difficult for equitable distribution of the country's resources for country-wide development. This is a threat to human security. As the electorate threatened to vote non-performing elected officials out of office in future elections, the collateral damage could be enormous. This could even include MPs who, though may have promising platforms, are voted out of office because they could not overcome the structural impediments and secure the development funding needed to embark on projects in their constituencies.

This structural problem has led some of the electorates to regret their choice of candidate. Consequently about 34 percent of Sierra Leoneans, a third of the population, regret their choices for public office.

Holding political tolerance workshops has been a routine in Sierra Leone since 2002. The government and international stakeholders are concern about the volatile political situation in the country and are working assiduously to resolve the issue. Consequently, it is counterintuitive for the ruling party in government to block developmental funding to Members of Parliament to create jobs, generate economic growth, and develop their constituencies. Since regionalism is entrenched in Sierra Leonean societies, it is less likely that such strategies could result in people switching from one party to another in the provinces. In fact it could further enhance entrenched regionalism. Denying funding to Members of Parliament for a likely switch from one party to the other not only denies the electorate the right to choose their preferred representative, it also affects the development of the communities in terms of the level of cooperation that could exist between the electorate and their representative. In Sierra Leone, elections are held every five years. The implication is that development of a community could be left behind for five years when the Member of Parliament's party is in the opposition. In the light of this, most Sierra Leoneans believe that the current governing system needs to be improved.

Issues of Civil Rights and Liberties

Sierra Leoneans generally believe that the government is sympathetic to issues of civil rights and liberties within the country. Government is seen as fairly tolerant with about 60 percent of Sierra Leoneans acknowledging the positive government initiative at promoting free speech. The proliferation of radio stations and prints media across the country are positive steps taken by the government to ensure secured civil liberties. On the other hand government closure of the opposition SLPP radio station in 2009 was a challenge to free speech and political tolerance. Majority of Sierra Leoneans also believe that the media in Sierra Leone is independent and free from government censorships. Media organizations are able to report on stories unhindered and which may include some hot-button issues that are critical of the government. However, about a third of Sierra Leoneans disagree that the media is independent. The Public Order Act, which enables the government to bring libel charges against media houses that broadcast or publish unsubstantiated critical report against the government and its institutions, is seen as a major issue to be worried about.

Embedded in democracy is government's responsiveness to the needs of the people. In states that are recovering from prolonged conflicts, such as that of Sierra Leone, the degree of government's responsiveness becomes very critical, especially when it was noted that apathy toward people's needs was one of the causes of the eleven-year conflict in the country. When asked if the government is currently reactive to the concerns of the people and reacting appropriately, about 59 percent of Sierra Leoneans agree that the government is reacting positively to the concerns of the people. Again about 82 percent of Sierra Leoneans agree that some government policies indicate that it is putting people's concerns into practice. They mention the gender policy, human rights policy, child rights bill, and the recent construction of roads to link Freetown to the provincial cities and other big towns, as evidence. These policies and initiatives are directed toward the broadening of rights and development.

Sierra Leoneans commend the role of the media in facilitating civil rights and liberties. The media has been instrumental in carrying people's concerns, and has also been the driving force in putting pressure on the government to consider developmental and other civil rights needs of the people. An overwhelming 91 percent of the respondents acknowledge that the media is instrumental in setting the agenda and shaping policies.

Oppression and human rights abuses characterized the period before and during the conflict in Sierra Leone. The legal system was dysfunctional, and only the few and the rich had access to the justice system and actually benefited from it. Backlog of cases were rampant, and many were denied the justice they desperately needed. One of the objectives of the justice sector reforms was to address the issue of case backlogs to ensure speedy adjudication of cases in order not to deny the Sierra Leonean people access to justice. When asked about the extent to which the legal system is handling litigations and other disputes, 56 percent of Sierra Leoneans agree that the courts are handling disputes quite well, while 44 percent disagree. This modest positive response could be explained by the lack of qualified lawyers in the country. Most of the courts are located in areas where they are not easily accessible to about 70 percent of the people. Most people, therefore, prefer to take disputed cases to the chiefs who are always accessible and use the tribal council to adjudicate different forms of disputes. This situation needs to be addressed so that a uniform law is applicable to all people equitably within Sierra Leonean societies. Generally, 66 percent agree that the legal system is effective in dealing with disputes, while 44 percent disagree.

Critical to the issues of civil rights and liberties is the rule of law which, according to the Sierra Leonean people, needs extensive improvements. The court's inability to adjudicate cases has led to an excessive adjournment of cases. This usually results from either the unavailability of logistics, such as vehicles or security personnel needed to transport the accused to court buildings, or the lack of defense lawyers and judges to handle cases. People who are alleged to have committed crimes have to wait for an uncertain long period of time before their cases are properly heard. This phenomenon violates the civil rights and liberties of people and also raises a serious human security concern. In the post-conflict era, this is a priority and the Sierra Leonean government needs to quickly address this situation. Governments could request logistical assistance from neighboring states to deal with the shortfall in logistics. When necessary, Sierra Leone could seek legal assistance from states such as Nigeria and Ghana who have abundant lawyers and judges to assist to reduce case backlogs.

Sierra Leoneans are of the opinion that citizens also have a role to play in ensuring that civil rights and liberties are enhanced within the various communities. Regular local forums to discuss civil rights and liberties issues are important. Sierra Leoneans understand that these rights and liberties are sometimes difficult to be realized, unless the people demand that government develop, implement, and also enforce them. Such local forums will act as educational forums where people will learn about their rights and liberties. Other initiatives, such as adherence to existing laws, reporting civil rights abuses to the appropriate institutions, and becoming tolerant to the needs of other diverse groups are some of the means by which the Sierra Leonean people can help entrench the respect of civil rights and liberties with Sierra Leonean societies.

PERSONAL SECURITY IN POST-CONFLICT SIERRA LEONE

In post-conflict states, the issue of personal security becomes imperative especially when tensions already exist between groups. Governments can choose to ignore situations when members of its own ethnic or auxiliary groups commit violence against other groups. On the other hand, when other groups commit violent acts on ethnic groups affiliated with the government, the government reacts violently toward the perpetrators. These strategies underlie the core of life and survival of the groups within the societies and have therefore become unwritten or latent institutions. Thus, the triggers are present and everyone is watching for these triggers to measure the level of societal security.

Safety of communities invariably leads to the security of the state and the entire region. Personal security is one of the components of human security, and it measures how safe people are in their persons within their respective communities. Ensuring personal security in the post-conflict is one of the expectations of the Sierra Leonean people. This is beneficial to both the government and the people, in that a secured environment facilitates the abilities of both the government and the people to plan and engage in developmental activities. Overall, majority of Sierra Leoneans (about 86 percent) agree that personal security within the country has improved and that government's efforts at improving the security sector account for the improvement in personal security. Sierra Leoneans also acknowledge that the security sector reforms that have ensured adequate education and training to the Sierra Leonean police have resulted in fair enforcement of the rule of law in all circumstances. Sierra Leoneans also see the decentralization of the security sector from the national, provincial, district, and down to the chiefdoms as a step in the right direction. They, however, noted that more security partnerships between the government and the people are needed. There are concerns about the lack of logistics (vehicles and equipments) for the police which make the police services' job difficult. The people recognize the fact that they have a role to play to ensure the enhancement of personal security. Civic responsibilities such as reporting any potential threat to security in the community to the appropriate government agency, establishing neighborhood forums to educate people on security issues, strengthening police/community partnerships, and internalizing the culture of tolerance are critical to personal security and a secured state.

ECONOMIC AND CASH FLOW SECURITY

With job creation and job security becoming increasingly elusive in the contemporary global world economy, requiring governments in post-conflict states to create and establish job security is a daunting task. However, job and cash-flow security are exactly the essence of economic security in the post-conflict. Cash-flow security is the perception and opportunity that exist which enables someone to have access to cash to cover at least the basic needs for the day.

The UNDP has noted that a significant percentage of available jobs are temporary and short-term basis. Accordingly, the UNDP has also noted that one significant consequence of this global job trend is the continual reduction in household incomes which have negative impacts on poverty levels. Thus the goal of achieving a positive economic outlook merely through job creation is not enough. The target should be the level of cash flow which, to a large extent, impacts the poverty levels. Cash-flow security is dependent on the job opportunities available both in the formal and informal sectors of the economy. In an African setting, cash-flow security could be viewed as the ease with which the opportunity exists for, for instance, a farmer, when the need be, to be able to take a day off his work at the farm, and be able to secure a day labor job to augment the family income. In the cities and towns, we are looking at a situation where the opportunity exists for someone with a regular job, and when the need be, could secure a part-time job in the evening or weekend to augment the family income.

The creation of employment opportunities was one of the important issues for peace consolidation in Sierra Leone as the end the war approached.

The Abidjan and the Lome Peace Accords had provisions that addressed job opportunities for the ex-combatants so as to keep their idle hands busy, enhance their economic security, and improve the general development of the country. However, job creation has been elusive in Sierra Leone since 2002. Many analysts view the high unemployment rate, especially among the youth, as a "ticking time bomb." Most Sierra Leonean youth are still unemployed and idle around street corners in Freetown and other major Provincial cities and towns. The 2003 national youth policy, numerous capacity building workshops across the country, and the DDR program have not resulted in the anticipated economic security targets. Thus job opportunities, for the most part, seem elusive in Sierra Leone. However, vast arable land lay idle and has since not been effectively exploited. The government's effort at making agriculture attractive to the youth has not been successful. The youth continue to move from the rural to the urban areas in search of non-existent jobs.

Public sector jobs are difficult to secure. Most Sierra Leoneans believe employment with the public service is not worth pursuing since it is difficult, if not impossible. Also, due to the high labor turnover in public service jobs during a change of government, such jobs even when secured are unsustainable. In some instances one has to be a loyal party member to be considered for a vacant position in the public service. This patronage system of rewarding party loyalists with jobs has politicized the public sector jobs and poses a serious human security threat not just to the Sierra Leonean worker but also to the development of the country as a whole. Patronage system eliminates experience and skills which elements for efficiency and effectiveness of labor at the work place.

Sierra Leoneans have a positive view of the private sector. The perception is that the private sector is the engine for growth and development. They also see opportunities for people to establish their own businesses. The low level of income is a huge challenge for small businesses to overcome. One of the fast growing small businesses is the communication industry. Young people with small capital buy and sell cell phones top-ups (units) to make a living. Nongovernmental organizations (NGOs) are widely considered to be part of the private sector in Sierra Leone. NGOs have been a source of employment in Sierra Leone. However, those that are hired are close relatives or acquaintances to the owners of these NGOs. Most Sierra Leoneans do not earn enough to take care of the family. The cash flow is woefully inadequate. Economic security in post-conflict Sierra Leone is not just pursuing job creation strategies but also cash-flow strategies. As the post-conflict peace is still fragile, cash-flow security could forestall the probability that rogue political elites will exploit the labor of idling youth to intimidate their political opponents. Government's efforts to create jobs have not been successful. Even the Chamber of Commerce has expressed concern about the lack of effort on the part of the government to create attractive incentives for investments in the agriculture sector.

Economic insecurity is the greatest human security threat in post-conflict Sierra Leone. It affects the school drop-out and illiteracy rates since parents do not have the financial means to enable their children to go to the universities and colleges. Other consequences include the culture of dependency, where people lose any enthusiasm regarding enterprise and entrepreneurship. Thus, acts of prostitution, violence, thefts, and other forms of armed robbery and civil disobedience become rampant.

Opportunities exist for the Sierra Leonean government to practically handle the issue of economic and cash-flow security. The government, in cooperation with private investors (local or foreign) and the Sierra Leonean people could form a tripartite co-op mechanized agricultural agency to exploit the huge arable land that is available in the country. The government, through the Ministry of Agriculture, and the private sector (possibly the Chamber of Commerce) can commit huge financial resources into the agriculture sector and make youth employment the target. Mechanized farming could have an attractive potential to the youth. Over time, the government could withdraw its participation and effectively entrust the agriculture sector into the hands of the private sector. When this is done successfully, it could be a more sustainable approach to cash-flow security and the overall development of the country.

CONCLUSION

Human security, the development and enforcement of institutions and processes that promote human empowerment and dignity, has important implications on issues of peace, stability, and development. It transcends just being a measure of development.[13] In post-conflict states, human security becomes the critical piece of the security/development puzzle and cannot be isolated from any discussions regarding sustainable peace and stability in the post-conflict era. Human security, therefore, becomes a tool and the driving force in the effort to secure sustainable peace and development in post-conflict states. Some have argued that development is the route for attaining human security.[14] Thus human security is seen as a dependent variable at the mercy of the development wand. Such a trickle down strategy could face major institutional challenges at achieving human security. Without effective institutions to guarantee human security, investments in development projects may be a wasteful endeavor. In most cases, while the appropriate question is asked regarding why targeted development levels have become elusive in the post-conflict, the response deviates from the question. Some post-conflict states and their donors have alternated between one type of development project to the other to boost growth and development. Because targeted outcomes have not been achieved we have had situations of donor fatigue, development stalemate, and extreme instability in some of these post-conflict states.

As this book discusses human security as an independent variable, it forces policymakers and other stakeholders not to apply "Band-Aid" strategies for development in the post-conflict era, but make sure that institutions that guarantee human security are put in place first before any attempt at sustainable development is initiated. Thus, attempts at pursuing any meaningful and sustainable peace in after-conflict states without first putting in place institutions and structures that effectively ensures human security is to "put the cart before the horse." In contemporary security discourse since the 1990s, it is the general consensus that pursuing national security though necessary is not insufficient to ensure the attainment of human security.[15] Human security is an all-encompassing concept.[16] It is a comprehensive approach and the components need to be addressed as a whole. This means that concentrating on just one of its component to the detriment of the others hinders the likelihood of achieving targeted goals. The discussion makes it clear that political leaders have incentive to create and be committed to institutional structures that promote human security since it, in turn, enhances elites' own security.[17]

Human security also transcends seemingly attractive government policy or strategy; human security is all about the people, and their perception regarding the effect of government policies in creating an enabling environment for people to achieve their projected individual goals and ultimately live a dignified life. People's perception of a positive environment has a strong positive relation with stability and development. In states recovering from conflict such as Sierra Leone, human security becomes much more imperative because people have high expectations and would like to see the impact of any reform reflect quickly. Because aspects of human security have not been achieved, there has been a drag on the reconstruction effort in Sierra Leone leading to a slow recovery and development.

Institutional reforms directed at human security have benefits both for Sierra Leone's political elites and citizens as the country transitions to a stable peace and development in the post-conflict era. This is an incentive to elites in the developing world who always dread insecurities to their political power. Political elites have a once-in-a-lifetime opportunity to establish institutions that determine the rules of the game regarding how things are done in the Sierra Leonean society. These reforms that are established could in fact enhance their economic survival long after they have left the political arena. These same reforms could enable them to stay clear of unethical and other corrupt behaviors for which they are usually hunted down once they leave office. On the part of the people, institutional reforms strengthen the trust and confidence they have in the leadership and the system as a whole which makes them active participants and supportive of subsequent government policies. There is clearly a disconnect between government policy and development in Sierra Leone. Human security accounts for such a gap.

The four human security pillars (political, civil, personal, and economic) discussed examine the reforms the Sierra Leonean government has put in place to address institutional challenges in the pursuit of peace, security, growth, and development. However, the analyses show that the reforms since 2002 have achieved minimal impact on development. The country still ranks among the lowest of any UNDP development indicators. The peace that currently exists in the country is very fragile. Sierra Leoneans viewed the election year 2012 as a defining moment for peace, stability, and growth in the country. Instead of focusing and engaging in how current government policies create the enabling environment for security and development, they hung their lives on election cycles. This is a challenge to the nation's leaders regarding the type of institutions and to what extent those institutions are creating enabling environment for people to develop themselves. This also raises questions regarding the process of stability in post-conflict states as well as other implications such as the essence of the relationship between human security, peace, and development.

In spite of the reforms in the civil and personal security, there are still concerns that the Sierra Leonean government needs to address. Though deteriorating civil and personal securities are prevalent in some seemingly stable developing states, in after-conflict states the stakes are higher. Post-Traumatic Stress Disorders (PTSD) have become one of the challenging consequences of war that military veterans, many of whom have been in the battle front for a long time, have to deal with. After eleven years of civil conflict and war fatigue in Sierra Leone, where every single family was affected, there is the likelihood that the society may have suffered from post-conflict stress and war disorders.[18] What makes it more precarious as compared to soldiers fighting on the battle ground is that this war is fought right in people's homes and backyards, market places, and churches. Even more serious is the fact that most of the perpetrators who committed heinous crimes during the war are neighbors who still live in the community as a result of the amnesty granted them.[19] Though a broader objective to attain security is important, even more imperative are the programs, logistics, and the political will to achieve those broad objectives. In some cases, targeted security goals are not achieved. The UNDP's strategy in tying security to development is a step in the right direction but targets are very difficult to realize.

External stakeholders are an important part of the effort at ensuring security in post-conflict Sierra Leone. However, it is the primary responsibility of the Sierra Leonean government to ensure that communities are secured especially when communities have accepted to reintegrate perpetrators of the civil conflict into the society. Blatant abuse of human rights by political leaders over the years, the lack of a clearly defined government plan regarding effective security policy, and the lack of government commitment to ensure security have a role to play in the deteriorating security situation that led to the conflict. In the post-conflict, the Sierra Leonean government needs to be fully committed to sustainable civil and personal security issues since the alternative would be the potential for violent conflict.

Reports of police reluctance to respond to certain crimes have been described as "isolated." These instances may honestly be isolated cases; however, they go a long way not only to hurt the reputation of the police, but also create serious personal security concerns. People's perception of the effectiveness of the police service becomes paramount in the post-conflict when the government needs to regain the confidence of the people regarding the extent to which it can use such governmental apparatus to ensure peace and security. A prominent community-based women's group in Makeni, Women Action for Human Dignity (WAHD), which organizes a radio broadcasts on security and human rights issues at the local radio station had to suspend its activities at the beginning of 2009 as a result of the threat to the lives of the women radio hosts.[20] The women's group claims that recent calls to the local police regarding domestic violence, rapes, and murder of women have not been investigated. Due to the insistent calls by these women on the radio program for the police to investigate into these personal security issues, they have consequently become targets. Perpetrators of such crimes have sent death threats to those women radio show hosts. As a temporary measure, the police provided escort services to the women in order to continue the radio program. Increases in armed robbery and violence across the country are an indication that the issue of personal security is by no means a critical one and a human security concern.

During the arms for development program, the UNDP noted that most arms that were returned were very old and unserviceable. The concern was whether sophisticated and dangerous arms were still out there. It is also the reality that popular farm [economic] equipment such as machetes and axes were the most dangerous weapons that were used in the Sierra Leonean conflict. It was this farm equipment that were used to sever the limbs of fellow neighbors, and which have left an indelible mark of the conflict within Sierra Leonean societies.

On the issue of political security, the Sierra Leonean people have been politically sensitized on how they can use the political process to attract government attention and to steer the direction of government policies. However, politics at the national level impedes the effectiveness with which the Sierra Leonean people could use the political process to demand government responsiveness. Parties in government consistently put impediments in the way of the opposition, making it difficult for the opposition to secure funding for developmental efforts in their respective constituencies.

Political intolerance continues to plague the peace and security in the country. Political factions occasionally destroy offices and other properties of their rivals. For instance, in March 2009, a dedication of the town clock in the center of Freetown led to the destruction of Sierra Leonean People's Party's office in Freetown. The UNDP quickly organized a peace workshop for the two leading political parties (SLPP and APC). Burning and destroying opponent party's assets are common place. Sudden outbursts of violence as a result of political intolerance are common even in the other provinces. Peace workshops have not ceased in Sierra Leone since 2002.

Youth unemployment has spiraled out of control and the government is having a difficult time in addressing the issue. In all, this is the most significant threat to human security that the government faces. The government of Sierra Leone needs to heed to calls from the Chamber of Commerce to pass investments laws that make the agriculture sector attractive, and which also could have positive effect on the youth unemployment issue. The country has huge arable land that it can take advantage of by instituting a tripartite arrangement involving the government, private sector, and the youth in some sort of an attractive mechanized farming. Currently in Sierra Leone, there is an unbalanced distribution of labor which has resulted in the movement of the strong and virile young men and women to the urban areas looking for non-existing jobs, while there is a shortage of the much-needed labor in the rural areas for agriculture activities.

The politics of public sector employment also take a toll on labor efficiency and effectiveness. Experienced staffs are removed from the public service due to their political affiliations. Sierra Leone needs all available resources, including experienced manpower, to pull through the peace, growth, and developmental challenges. Consequently, the Sierra Leonean government continues to struggle in the efforts at sustainable peace and development. Fundamental institutional structures that ensure human security have not been fully put in place, and an effective enabling environment is yet to be established.

NOTES

1. Commonly known as the Arab Spring, it is associated with massive demonstration and protest wave that swept through the Arab world beginning December 18, 2010
2. Security fatigue is a situation where global leaders, fully aware of the implications of domestic security to global security refuse to commit resources to assist in strengthening domestic security in other states.
3. This includes the existence of opportunities for people to establish their own small businesses.
4. A member of parliament or someone elected to a local council office.

5. See Sumit Ganguly. 1996. "Conflict and Crisis in South and Southwest Asia," in Michael Brown (ed.) *The International Dimensions of Internal Conflict*. Cambridge, MA: Massachusetts Institute of Technology Press, pp. 141–72; D.L. Horowitz. 1985. *Ethnic Groups in Conflict*. Berkeley: University of California Press. Also, A. Wimmer, et al. 2004. *Facing Ethnic Conflicts: Toward a New Realism*. Lanham, MD: Rowman & Littlefield Publishers, Inc.

6. These are people mostly from the elite's tribe or very close acquaintances.

7. See Bruce Bueno de Mesquita, et al. 2003. *The Logic of Political Survival*. Cambridge, MA: The Massachusetts Institute of Technology Press.

8. Bad governance is where political elites centralize political power and consciously close opportunities for citizens to participate in the governing process.

9. See Abdul Karim Bangura. 2007. "Politicized Ethnicities versus Tribal Ethnicities: Examples from Liberia, Rwanda, and Sierra Leone." In Santosh C. Saha (ed.) *The Politics of Ethnicity and National Identity*. New York: Peter Lang Publishing Inc., pp. 121–38.

10. DDR (Disarmament, Demobilization, and Reintegration).

11. This is with regard to taking part in the voting process during, general, provincial, district, and other local elections.

12. Elements of the political process include membership in a political party, engaging in campaigning, voting, engaging representatives during question times, ability to present self as candidates in elections, activities of civil society groups, engaging in political discussion without fear, etc.

13. See Amartya Sen. 1999. *Development as freedom*. New York: Anchor Books, pp. 37–40

14. See Mahbub ul Haq, "New Imperatives of Human Security," RGICS Paper # 17, Rajiv Gandhi Institute for Contemporary Studies (RGICS), Rajiv Gandhi Foundation, New Delhi, 1994, p.1.

15. See "Human Security: Safety for People in a Changing World," a paper prepared by the Department of Foreign Affairs and International Trade (DFAIT), http://www.dfait.maeci.gc.ca/foreignp/Human Security/secur-e.htm, p. 1.

16. See Zacarias, Agostinho. 2003. "Redefining Security." In *From Cape to Congo: Southern Africa's Evolving Security Challenges*. Mwesiga Baregu and Christopher Landsberg (eds.) Boulder: Lynne Rienner Publishers, Inc., p. 42. Also, Bryden, Alan, Timothy Donais, and Heiner Hanggi. 2005. *Shaping Security Governance Agenda in Post-Conflict Peacebuilding*. Geneva: Geneva Center for the democratic Control of Armed Forces.

17. Being rational human beings, elites' commitments are interest driven. However, establishing institutions that guarantee human security could enable elites to achieve their interests whatever those interests could be.

18. This involves the reliving of the war and other personal security issues that may impede people's effort at embracing the new reality of post-war era.

19. See the provisions in the Peace Accords signed in Abidjan and Lome as well as the DDR program on how to deal with ex-combatants.

20. This information was obtained from an interview with the head of WAHD in Makeni.

Bibliography

Abdullah, Ibrahim. 1997. "Bush Path to Destruction: The Origin and Character of the Revolutionary United Front." *African Development*. 22: 3–4.

Ake, Claude (ed.). 1985. "The State in Contemporary Africa." In *Political Economy of Nigeria*. London: Longman. p. 2.

Anti-Corruption Act, 2001.

Archibald, Steven, and Paul Richards. 2002. "Converts to Human Rights? Popular Debates about War and Justice in Rural Central Sierra Leone." *Africa*. Vol. 72 (3).

Aruna Turay. "In Sierra Leone, Vice-president Sam-Sumana Dismayed over slow Decentralization." Article appearing in the *Awareness Times* newspaper, Freetown. June 1, 2009.

Axworthy, Lloyd. 1997. "Canada and Human Security: The Need for leadership." *International Journal*, Vol. 52, pp. 183–96.

Baker, Bruce. 2005. "Who Do People Turn to for Policing in Sierra Leone?" *Journal of Contemporary African Studies*, Vol. 23 (3), (September) pp. 371–90.

Bangura, Abdul Karim. 2007. "Politicized Ethnicities versus Tribal Ethnicities: Examples from Liberia, Rwanda, and Sierra Leone." In Santosh C. Saha (ed.) *The Politics of Ethnicity and National Identity*. New York: Peter Lang Publishing Inc., pp. 121–38.

Berdal, Mats, and David M. Malone (eds.). 2000. *Greed and Grievance: Economic Agendas in Civil Wars*. Boulder, CO: Lynne Reinner Publishers, Inc.

Biddle, K. 2000. "Conflict, Security, and Development," *Group Bulletin*, March–April: 1–4.

Bryden, Alan, and Heiner Hanggi. 2005. *Security Governance in Post-Conflict Peacebuilding*. Piscataway, NJ: Transaction Publishers.

Bryden, Alan, Timothy Donais, and Heiner Hanggi. 2005. *Shaping Security Governance Agenda in Post-Conflict Peacebuilding*. Geneva: Geneva Center for the Democratic Control of Armed Forces.

Bryna, Hallam, "Local Council not Involving Citizens, Study Finds." Article appearing in the *Concord Times* (Freetown) in November 2008.

Bueno de Mesquita, Bruce, et al. 2003. *The Logic of Political Survival*. Cambridge: The Massachusetts Institute of Technology Press.

Bueno de Mesquita, Bruce. 1981. *The War Trap*. New Haven, CT: Yale University Press.

Collier, Paul, and Anke Hoeffler. 2000. *Greed and Grievance in Civil Wars*. Washington, DC: World Bank Development Research Group.

Collier, Paul, and Nicholas Sambanis (eds.). 2005. *Understanding Civil War (Volume 1: Africa): Evidence and Analysis*. Washington, DC: The World Bank.

Collier, Paul, Anke Hoeffler, and Dominic Rohner. 2006. "Beyond Greed and Grievance: Feasibility and Civil War," *Center for the Study of African Economies*, Working Paper. 10 (7) August 2006.

Commission on Human Security. 2003. *Human Security Now*. New York: Commission on Human Security.

Conteh-Morgan, Earl, and Mac Dixon-Fyle. 1999. *Sierra Leone at the End of the Twentieth Century: History, Politics, and Society*. New York: Peter Lang Publishing, Inc.

Copeland, Dale C. 1999. "Economic Interdependence and War: A Theory of Trade Expectation," *International Studies,* Vol. 20 No. 4 (Spring), pp. 5–41.

David, Wilfred I. 2004. *The Humanitarian Development Paradigm: Search for Global Justice*. Lanham, MD: University Press of America, Inc.

Dedring, Juergen. 2008. *The United Nations Security Council in the 1990s: Resurgence and Renewal.* Albany: State University of New York Press.

Department of Foreign Affairs and International Trade. 1999. "Human Security: Safety for People in a Changing World." A paper presented by Lloyd Axworthy, Minister of Foreign Affairs, in Ottawa, Canada, on April 29, 1999. http://www.cpdsindia.org/peopleinachangingworld.htm.

Downs, Anthony. 1957. *An Economic Theory of Democracy*. New York: Harper.

Dupuy, Kendra, and Helga Malmin Binningsbo. 2007. *Power-sharing and Peacebuilding in Sierra Leone: Power-sharing Agreements, Negotiations, and Peace Process*, CSCW papers, Center for the Study of Civil War, PRIO.

Enterline, A. J. 1998. "Regime Changes, Neighborhoods, and Interstate Conflict, 1816–1992." *Journal of Conflict Resolution*. 42: 804–29.

Esman, Milton. 2004. "Ethnic Pluralism: Strategies for Conflict Management." In *Facing Ethnic Conflicts: Toward a New Realism.* A. Wimmer, et al. (eds.). Lanham, MD: Rowman & Littlefield Publishers, Inc.

Evans, Tony. 2005. *The Politics of Human Rights: A Global Perspective*. London: Pluto Press.

Fearon, James D. 1995. "Rationalists Explanations for War." *International Organization*, Vol. 49, No. 3 (Summer 1995), pp. 379–414.

Fearon, James D., and David D. Laitin. "Ethnicity, Insurgency, and Civil War" *American Political Science Review* 97, 1 (Feb 2003): pp. 75–79.

Fischer, Horst, and Noelle Quenivet (eds.). 2005. *Post-Conflict Reconstruction: Nation and/or State-Building*. Berlin: BWV, Berliner Wissenschafts-Verlag.

Florini, A. and P.J. Simmons. 1998. *The New Security Thinking: A Review of the North American Literature.* New York: Carnegie Endowment for International Peace.

Fukuyama, Francis. 2004. *State-building: Governance and World Order in the 21st Century*. Ithaca, NY: Cornell University Press.

Ganguly, R. and Taras R.C. 1998. *Understanding Ethnic Conflict: The International Dimension.* New York: Addison-Wiley Educational Publishers Inc.

Ganguly, Sumit. 1996. "Conflict and Crisis in South and Southwest Asia," in Michael Brown (ed.), *The International Dimensions of Internal Conflict.* Cambridge: Massachusetts Institute of Technology Press, pp. 141–72.

Gershoni, Yekutiel. 1997. "War without End and an End to War: The Prolonged Wars in Liberia and Sierra Leone." *African Studies Review*, Vol. 40, No. 3 (December), pp. 55–76.

Gibrill, Hashim. 2007. "The Disintegration and Restoration of State Authority in Sierra Leone" In *Beyond State failure and Collapse: Making the State Relevant in Africa.* George Klay Kieh Jr. (ed.). Lanham, MD: Lexington Books.

Gleditsch, Nils Peter, H. Hegre, Tanja Ellingsen, and Scott Gates. 2001. "Toward a Democratic Civil Peace? Democracy, Political Change and Civil War, 1816–1992." *American Political Science Review* 95 (1): 33–47.

Government of Sierra Leone: Justice Sector Reform Strategy and Investment Plan (2008-2010); Vision: "A Sierra Leone where there is safety for people, security of property, and access to property." Document drafted in 2007.

Government of Sierra Leone: Sierra Leone National Youth Policy. 2002. Published by the UNDP.

Government of Sierra Leone: The Local Court Act, 1963.

Government of Sierra Leone: The Local Government Act of Sierra Leone. Enacted by an Act of Parliament in March 2004. *A supplement to the Sierra Leone Gazette Extraordinary- Vol. CXXXIV, No. 14.*

Government of Sierra Leone: The National Security and Central Intelligence Act. Enacted by the President and Members of Parliament in July 2002. *A supplement to the Sierra Leone Gazette Extraordinary, Vol. CXXXIV, No. 42.*

Haq, Mahbub ul. 1994. "New Imperatives of Human Security," RGICS Paper No. 17, Rajiv Gandhi Institute for Contemporary Studies. New Delhi: Rajiv Gandhi Foundation.

Harbeson, John. 2008. "Power Sharing Pacts Have Not Worked Well in Africa." March 8. http://allafrica.com/stories/200803310319.html.

Harff, Barbara, and Ted Gurr. 1994. *Ethnic Conflict in World Politics*. Boulder, CO: Westview Press.

Henderson, E. A. 2002. *Democracy and War: The End of an Illusion?* Boulder, CO: Lynne Rienner Publishers, Inc.

Hirsch, John L. 2001. *Sierra Leone: Diamonds and the Struggle for Democracy.* Boulder, CO: Lynne Rienner Publishers, Inc.

Horowitz, D.L. 1985. *Ethnic Groups in Conflict*. Berkeley: University of California Press.

Horowitz, Donald. 2004. "Some Realism about Constitutional Engineering." In *Facing Ethnic Conflicts: Toward a New Realism.* A. Wimmer, et al. (eds.) Lanham, MD: Rowman & Littlefield Publishers, Inc., pp. 245–57.

Human Security Report 2005: War and Peace in the 21st Century. New York: Oxford University Press.

Kandeh, Jimmy D. 1995. "Sierra Leone: Contradictory Class Functionality of the 'Soft' State." *Review of African Political Economy*. 22 (55).

Kaplan, Robert D. 2000. *The Coming Anarchy: Shattering the Dreams of the Post-Cold War.* New York: Random House Inc.

Keen, David. 2000. "Incentives and Disincentives for Violence" In *Greed and Grievance: Economic Agendas in Civil Wars.* Mats Berdal and David M. Malone. (eds.). Boulder, CO: Lynne Reinner Publishers, Inc.

Kieh Jr., George Klay (ed.). 2007. *Beyond State failure and Collapse: Making the State Relevant in Africa.* Lanham, MD: Lexington Books.

Kpundeh, Sahr J. 1993. "Elites, Non-Elites and Corruption: An Attitudinal Analysis of Data from Sierra Leone." Ph.D. dissertation. Howard University.

Krishna, Anirudh et al. (eds.). 1997. *Reasons for Hope: Instructive Experiences in Rural Development.* Herndon, VA: Kumarian Press.

Lake, Anthony. 1993, September 21. *From Containment to Enlargement*. Typescript. Baltimore: School of Advanced International Studies, John Hopkins University, pp. 1–14.

Lake, David A. and Donald Rothchild. 1996. "Containing Fear: The Origins and Management of Ethnic Conflict." *International Security*, Vol. 21, No. 2 (autumn), pp. 41–75.

Laremont, Rene Ricardo, and Fouad Kalouche (eds.). 2002. *Africa and Other Civilizations: Conquest and Conquest-Conquest*. Trenton, NJ: Africa World Press, Inc.

Lemarchand, Rene. 1995. *Burundi: Ethnic Conflict and Genocide*. New York: Wilson Center Press.

Leonard, David, and Scott Straus. 2003. *Africa's Stalled Development: International Causes and Cures*. Boulder, CO: Lynne Rienner Publishers, Inc.

Lijphart, Arend. 1977. *Democracy in Plural Societies*. New Haven, CT: Yale University Press.

Mamdani, Mahmood. 1992. "The Peasant Question and the Contemporary Question." In Kennett, David and Tukumbi Lumumba-Kasongo (eds.) *Structural Adjustment and the Crisis in Africa: Economic and Political Perspective*. New York: The Edwin Mellen Press.

Mansfield, E. D., and Jack Snyder. 1995. "Democratization and the Dangers of War." *International Security*. 20:5–38.

Mansfield, E. D., and Jack Snyder. 2002. "Incomplete Democratization and the Outbreak of Military Disputes." *International Studies Quarterly*. 46:529–49.

Mariama Kandeh, "Sierra Leone: Youth Unemployment—A Time Bomb." Article appearing in the *Concord Times* (Freetown) in July 1, 2008.

Mazrui, Ali. 1999. "African Security: The Erosion of the State and the Decline of Race as a Basis for Human Relations." In *Globalization, Human Security and the African Experience*. Caroline Thomas and Peter Wilkin (eds.). Boulder, CO: Lynne Rienner publishers, Inc.

Mazrui, Ali. 2002. "The Frankenstein State and the International Order." In Laremont, Rene Ricardo, and Fouad Kalouche, eds. *Africa and Other Civilizations: Conquest and Conquest-Conquest.* Trenton, NJ: Africa World Press, Inc.

Meek, Sarah. 2003. "Policing Sierra Leone." In M. Malan, S. Meek, T. Thusi, J. Ginifer, and P. Coker (eds.). *Sierra Leone: Building the Road to Recovery.* Monograph 80. Pretoria: Institute for Security Studies.

Mohamed Massaquoi, "Sierra Leone: Opinion—Chieftaincy Reforms and the Role of Governance." Article appearing in the *Concord Times* (Freetown). March 18, 2009.

Mosha, Felix. 2005. "Mediation and Mediators of the Conflicts in the Great Lakes Region (GLR)". In *Africa Conflict, Peace and Governance Monitor, 2005.* Ibadan: Dokun Publishing House. pp. 127–46.

Moss, Todd; Gunilla Pettersson; and Nicholas van de Walle. 2006. "An Aid-Institution Paradox? A Review Essay on Aid Dependency and State Building in sub-Saharan Africa." In *Working Paper 74.* Washington, DC: Center for Global Development.

Mwanasali, Musifiky. 2000. "The View from Below" In Mats Berdal and David M. Malone (eds.). *Greed and Grievance: Economic Agendas in Civil Wars.* Boulder, CO: Lynne Reinner Publishers, Inc., pp. 137–53.

National Geographic: "Blood Diamonds." Film.

O'Flynn, I., and Donald Russell (ed.) 2005. *Power-Sharing: Institutional and Social Reform in Divided Societies.* London: Pluto Press.

Orr, Robert (ed.). 2004. *Winning the Peace: An American Strategy for Post Conflict Reconstruction.* Washington, DC: CSIS Press.

Ouedraogo, Youssouf. "The African Union and Conflict Resolution" *In African Geopolitics* No. 24, October–December 2006, pp. 23–41.

Paris, Roland. 2004. *At Wars End: Building Peace After Civil Conflict.* New York: Cambridge University Press.

Posen, Barry R. 1993. "The Security Dilemma and Ethnic Conflict." In Michael E. Brown (ed.) *Ethnic Conflict and International Security.* Princeton: Princeton University Press.

Pozzoni, Barbara and Nalini Kumar. 2005. "A Review of the Literature on Participatory Approaches to Local Development for an Evaluation of the Effectiveness of the World Bank Support for Community-Based and Driven Development Approaches." *Operations Evaluation Department.* Washington, DC: The World Bank.

Rashid, Ishmael. 1997. "Subaltern Theory and Youth Crisis." *African Development.* 22: 3–4.

Renner, Michael. 1998. "The Global Divide: Socio-economic Disparities and International Security." In Michael Klare and Yogesh Chandrani (eds.) *World Security: Challenges for a New Century,* 3rd ed. New York: St. Martins Press. pp. 273–94.

Reno, William. 1995. *Corruption and State Politics in Sierra Leone.* New York: Cambridge University Press.

Reno, William. 1998. *Warlord Politics and the African State.* Boulder, CO: Lynne Rienner Publishers, Inc.

Reno, William. 2000. "Shadow States and the Political Economy of Civil Wars" In *Greed and Grievance: Economic Agendas in Civil Wars.* Berdal, Mats, and David M. Malone (eds.) Boulder, CO: Lynne Reinner Publishers, Inc.

Richards, Paul. 1996. *Fighting for the Rain Forest: War, Youth and Resources in Sierra Leone.* London: Villiers Publications.

Richards, Paul. 2001. "Are 'Forest' Wars in Africa Resource Conflicts? A Case of Sierra Leone" In *Violent Environments.* Nancy Lee Peluso and Michael Watts (eds.) Ithaca, NY: Cornell University Press.

Roeder, P. G., and Donald Rothchild, Ed. 2005. *Sustainable Peace: Power and Democracy after Civil Wars.* Ithaca, NY: Cornell University Press.

Rothchild, Donald. 2004. "Liberalism, Democracy, and Conflict Management: The African Experience." In *Facing Ethnic Conflicts: Toward a New Realism.* A. Wimmer, et al. (eds.) Lanham, MD: Rowman & Littlefield Publishers, Inc., pp. 226–44.

Russett, Bruce M. and John R. Oneal. 2001. *Triangulating Peace: Democracy, Interdependence, and International Organization.* New York: Norton.

Salim, Ahmed Salim. 2002. *African Conflicts: Their Management, Resolution and Post-Conflict Reconstruction.* Addis Ababa: Development Policy Management Forum.
Sambanis, Nicholas. 2001. "Do Ethnic and Nonethnic Civil Wars Have the Same Causes? A Theoretical and Empirical Inquiry (Part 1)." *The Journal of Conflict Resolution*, Vol. 45, No. 3 (June), pp. 259–82.
Sayoh Kamara, "APC Detractors want to destroy one of Salone's Success Stories." Article appearing in *Awareness Times* newspaper, Freetown. October 15, 2009.
Sen, Amartya. 1999. *Development as Freedom*. New York: Anchor Books.
Sierra Leone Court Monitoring Program (SLCMP): "After you have been arrested; what next." A booklet initially printed in 2007 with the support from the Special Court of Sierra Leone.
Sierra Leone Truth and Reconciliation Commission (TRC). 2004. "Witness to Truth: Report of the Sierra Leone Truth and Reconciliation Commission (Provisional)." Freetown: TRC.
Stedman, S. J., Donald Rothchild, and Elizabeth Consens. 2002. *Ending Civil Wars: The Implementation of Peace Agreements*. Boulder, CO: Lynne Rienner Publishers, Inc.
Stevens, Siaka Probyn. 1984. *What Life Has Taught Me: The Autobiography of President Siaka Stevens of Sierra Leone.* London: Kensal Press.
Sweetman, Caroline. 2005. *Gender, Peace-Building, and Reconstruction.* Oxford: Oxfam.
Thakur, R., and E. Newman (eds.) 2004. *Broadening Asia's Security and Discourse Agenda*, Tokyo: United Nations University Press.
The Abidjan Peace Accord, 1996: A peace agreement between the government of Sierra Leone and the Revolutionary United Front of Sierra Leone.
The Lome Peace Accord, 1999: A peace agreement between the government of Sierra Leone and the Revolutionary United Front of Sierra Leone.
The Monitor: Weekly magazine published by SLCMP.
Thomas, Caroline, and Peter Wilkin (eds.) 1999. *Globalization, Human Security and the African Experience.* Boulder, CO: Lynne Rienner Publishers, Inc.
Tickner, Ann. 2004. "Feminist Responses to International Security." *Peace Review* 16 (1): 43–48.
UNDP Sierra Leone. Arms for Development. End of Year Progress report. 2007.
United Nations Development Program: Human Development Report, 1994.
Voice of America News article, April 2008: Opposition Strike Falters in Zimbabwe. http://www1.voanews.com/english/news/a-13-2008-04-15-voa61-66747377.html.
Wallerstein, Immanuel. 2004. *World Systems Analysis: An Introduction*. Durham, NC: Duke University Press.
Wimmer, A. et al. 2004. *Facing Ethnic Conflicts: Toward a New Realism*. Lanham, MD: Rowman & Littlefield Publishers, Inc.
World Bank. 1998. *Post-Conflict Reconstruction: The Role of the World Bank.* Washington, DC: World Bank.
Zacarias, Agostinho. 2003. "Redefining Security." In *From Cape to Congo: Southern Africa's Evolving Security Challenges.* Mwesiga Baregu and Christopher Landsberg (eds.) Boulder, CO: Lynne Rienner Publishers, Inc., pp. 31–52.

Index

About the Author

Francis Wiafe-Amoako is lecturer at the University of Toronto and Ryerson University, independent consultant at the International Center for Capacity Development, and director of the Center for Sustained Domestic Security and Development. The center's main goal is the development of unique and viable institutions for stability and development. His research focuses on migration and security, conflict management and post-conflict stability, and institutional design. He holds a Bachelor of Commerce degree from the University of Cape Coast, Ghana; Master of Arts degrees from East Stroudsburg University and Binghamton University (SUNY); and a PhD from Howard University in Washington, D.C. His teaching career has spanned the fields of international relations and security, international development, peace negotiations, comparative political institutions, and politics of the global south. He has taught at the University of Toronto and Ryerson University in Canada, Samford University in Birmingham, Alabama, and Montgomery College in Rockville, Maryland.

Lightning Source UK Ltd.
Milton Keynes UK
UKOW05n1815220714

235569UK00006B/66/P

9 780739 191330